CW00550671

Play, naturally

Play, naturally

A review of children's natural play

Stuart Lester and Martin Maudsley
Playwork Partnerships

NCB promotes the voices, interests and well-being of all children and young people across every aspect of their lives.

As an umbrella body for the children's sector in England and Northern Ireland, we provide essential information on policy, research and best practice for our members and other partners.

NCB aims to:

- challenge disadvantage in childhood
- work with children and young people to ensure they are involved in all matters that affect their lives
- promote multidisciplinary cross-agency partnerships and good practice
- influence government policy through policy development and advocacy
- undertake high quality research and work from an evidence-based perspective
- disseminate information to all those working with children and young people, and to children and young people themselves.

NCB has adopted and works within the UN Convention on the Rights of the Child.

Published for Play England by the National Children's Bureau

National Children's Bureau, 8 Wakley Street, London EC1V 7QE
Tel: 020 7843 6000
Website: www.ncb.org.uk
Registered charity number: 258825

NCB works in partnership with Children in Scotland (www.childreninscotland.org.uk) and Children in Wales (www.childreninwales.org.uk).

Play England is part of the National Children's Bureau and is supported by the Big Lottery Fund

© Play England 2007

ISBN: 978-1-905818-15-0

British Library Cataloguing in Publication Data
A catalogue record for this book is available from the British Library.

All rights reserved. No part of this publication may be reproduced, stored in a retrieval system or transmitted in any form by any person without the written permission of the publisher.

The views expressed in this book are those of the authors and not necessarily those of the National Children's Bureau.

Contents

Contents

Acknowledgements

This research was commissioned to support Playday 2006: *Play, naturally*.

Playday is the annual celebration of children's right to play. The national campaign involves thousands of children and young people getting out to play at locally organised events. Playday events range from small-scale neighbourhood get-togethers to large-scale public events organised by local authorities and national organisations.

The Playday 2006 theme, *Play, naturally*, was chosen in recognition of children's natural playfulness and acknowledged the variety and stimulation that natural spaces and elements offer for play. The campaign also highlighted that opportunities for children to play in natural spaces are in serious decline.

Playday is coordinated by Play England, part of the National Children's Bureau, working in partnership with PlayBoard Northern Ireland, Play Scotland and Play Wales.

For more information about Playday, visit www.playday.org.uk

This review was written by Stuart Lester and Martin Maudsley for Playwork Partnerships, which is based at the University of Gloucestershire.

Stuart Lester

Stuart Lester has worked for many years in a variety of play projects and is currently Senior Lecturer in Playwork at the University of Gloucestershire and an Independent Playwork Trainer and Adviser.

Martin Maudsley

Martin Maudsley works part-time for Playwork Partnerships as their Outdoor Play Development Officer, supporting and developing opportunities for children to play in outdoor spaces and with natural elements. Martin also works as a trainer and playworker (with Swainswick Explorers) and has an enduring passion for wild adventures in wild spaces.

Image credits

Cover	Martin Maudsley/Swainswick Explorers www.playingoutdoors.co.uk
Page ii	Martin Maudsley
Page xii	Play England/Philip Wolmuth
Page 1	Faith Bennett
Page 8	Play England/Philip Wolmuth
Page 9	Martin Maudsley/Swainswick Explorers www.playingoutdoors.co.uk
Page 23	Play England (Evergreen Adventure Playground)
Page 50	Play England/Philip Wolmuth (Somerford Grove Adventure Playground)
Page 51	Play England/Philip Wolmuth
Page 68	Play England (Evergreen Adventure Playground)
Page 69	Martin Maudsley
Page 124	Play England/Philip Wolmuth (Somerford Grove Adventure Playground)

Childhood memories

Stuart Lester: the hills

There was a patch of land that separated the edge of the council estate from the new housing developments that were rapidly expanding into the countryside of the surrounding areas. This land grew from a tipping site for excavations – and very quickly became overgrown. This was a prominent site for play throughout my childhood, and assumed the rather imaginative name of 'the hills'.

This piece of land remained untouched throughout my childhood – a 'border' between the old and the new – and became a favourite place for playing out. For many children from the estate the hills provided a meeting place, somewhere to go where it was likely that other children from the immediate area would also be. The steep slopes of the hills lent themselves to all kinds of activity: sliding down on boards, rolling, and riding bikes and go-carts at speed. The sides of the hills were excavated to make dens and shelters, places where children told jokes and stories, moaned about parents and school – or just lay around in the grass 'doing nothing'. As the summer months wore on, the grass grew taller and became cover for playing hide-and-seek games and all kinds of heroic adventures and intrigues.

The place became invested with meanings, both good and bad. It held multiple 'playlines' – an intricate network of uses, legends and memories, invisible but known to every child within the local area. These playlines remained hidden from adults, who were generally indifferent to the value that such space afforded.

Martin Maudsley: the lane

There was a green lane amongst semi-detached houses that led – physically and metaphorically – from suburban orderliness to wild playfulness. It formed one of my earliest memories of place and play. As a neglected wasteland it was a precious wonderland to me and my cohort of street-mates of treasures, encounters and stories. The weather, the seasons and time subtly changed the playful qualities of the lane, but it was equally our inner variability as children that helped create the unending diversity of play. The lane's landscape sent out playful invitations, which only we could detect – and often they were offered only once. We grabbed them while we could.

As we grew in size and confidence we travelled further down the lane: we stayed out longer, we came home dirtier, we took bigger risks, our play became more febrile, and we became more secretive about our places and actions. The lane was wide enough and wild enough to hold all our bold playfulness; whilst we were children it remained unfathomable, impenetrable, incomprehensible.

What the research in this book clearly indicates is that children want and need access to the same wild spaces – the 'hills' and 'lanes' – that we recall from our childhoods, the local natural spaces that remain seemingly unkempt and messy, that children can claim and use as their own, and that allow them to become immersed in nature in all its forms and manifestations.

Nature is extremely resilient to children's playful use. Also, we suggest, through playing in natural environments children themselves have the potential to become highly resilient. Playing naturally is not simply contained in a precious sense of caring for the environment, but as a real and immediate experience of playing uninhibitedly among the diversity and potential that such spaces afford. Where there is compatibility between children's play needs and the opportunities offered by a place, there are likely to be strong affective relationships.

Although natural landscapes and children's natures remain inherently playful, children's 'field of free action' – their ability to discover and accept nature's invitations – is shrinking rapidly. It is perhaps this issue that represents the fundamental change over time in children's relationship to outdoor spaces. Of course, many children may still find spaces to call their own and consequent brief occasions to play freely, but others struggle to reap the benefits from interacting independently with wildness. Research would suggest that a number of significant and interconnected factors are contributing to this situation, which is discussed at some length in this book, particularly the prevailing sense that the outdoors is a place of danger and threat to children.

One of this book's fundamental messages is the value and importance of nearby nature, for children's play in particular and for human health and well-being in general. Therefore we need to ensure that our human environments allow the natural habitats of children to survive and thrive. Indeed, the very survival of natural spaces in the future may well depend on providing children with opportunities to play naturally today.

Stuart Lester and Martin Maudsley
October 2007

Foreword

Living on junk food and sugary drinks, entertained exclusively by television, DVDs, computer games and the internet, today's children, it seems, have no interest in the outdoors.

Research challenges this popular view that children are hooked on modern technology and sedentary, indoor pastimes. A survey, commissioned in August 2006 by Play England, for Playday – the annual celebration of children's right to play – found that 86 per cent of children prefer outdoor activities, including playing out with their friends, building dens and getting muddy, to playing computer games and the like; and 82 per cent said that their favourite places to play were natural spaces, such as gardens, parks and local fields.

The contents of this book, drawn from a research review published by Play England at the same time, suggests that there is substantial evidence that children have a strong and deep-rooted sensitivity to the natural world and that play, a biologically driven instinct, is the primary mechanism through which they encounter and explore their immediate physical environment. Children play instinctively with natural elements – they are natural experts.

As such, play is the process whereby children fulfil their drive to affiliate with nature, and natural environments provide the best settings for children to engage and actualise their deep need to play.

The review found that there is significant evidence to support the assertion that there are wide-ranging values and benefits arising from children's play in natural settings. However, the review went on to identify that there are now very significant and wide-ranging barriers to children enjoying these benefits, and that opportunities for children to access and play freely in natural spaces are seriously compromised. This is due to a variety of interconnected factors.

To ensure that today's children are able to enjoy and experience the benefits of play in natural settings, the review proposed some principles and priorities for action. Importantly, local authority play strategies should clearly acknowledge the importance of natural play and natural play spaces to enhance children's play lives; access to nature needs to be protected and developed; the design of outdoor spaces should support natural play by incorporating successful practice and research principles, and a consistent approach to environmental play provision must be developed via sustainable funding, training, networking and strategic support.

As lottery funding brings increased investment and as local authorities are asked to be more strategic in planning for play, there are opportunities for all parts of the play sector to look afresh at how provision can meet all children's deep and enduring need to experience and interact with nature.

At a time of growing alarm both at the constraints and pressures on childhood and at the damage being done to the planet by the modern world, giving back to children the chance to enjoy and nurture their affinity with nature is one of the most important challenges of our time.

Adrian Voce
Director of Play England
October 2007

Executive summary

Evidence and information collated in this review supports the following key findings.

Children's natures

- Extensive research shows that children have a strong and deep-rooted sensitivity to the natural world. Whilst there is evidence to support that this is biologically determined, other perspectives recognise the interplay of genes, individuals and environment in the expression of this attachment.
- The human relationship with the natural world is complex. The distinction between nature and human-made is a relatively new concept, reflecting significant changes to the physical, social, cultural, economic and political landscape. Any attempt to explore children's relationship with the natural world must take into account all of the above dimensions.
- For children, play is a biological drive and the primary mechanism through which they encounter and explore their immediate physical environments. Children play instinctively with natural elements; they are natural experts.

  As such: play is the process whereby children fulfil their drive to affiliate with nature, and natural environments provide optimal settings for children to engage and actualise their drive to play.

The values and benefits of children's play in natural settings

- There is substantial evidence that supports the wide-ranging values and benefits arising from children's play in natural settings. The research allows for some important conclusions about the relationship between children's play and natural environments to be drawn:
  - Natural environments support a wide range of children's play. The diverse, dynamic and flexible features that can be found in natural spaces afford opportunities for extensive intentional play behaviours.
  - Whilst children do not necessarily differentiate between natural and artificial elements in their play, predominantly natural outdoor settings are more likely to be perceived by children as free from adult agendas and thus more open to the possibilities of play.
  - Playing in natural spaces offers possibilities for: control and mastery, construction of special spaces, manipulating loose parts, different ways of moving, risk-taking etc. Childhood experiences of playing with nature also instil a sense of wonder, stimulating creativity, imagination and symbolic play.

- Children's opportunities to playfully access their immediate natural environments support the development of a sense of place and attachment. Playing in natural spaces also supports a child's sense of self, allowing children to recognise their independence alongside an interdependence and connectedness with their ecological worlds.
- The powerful combination of a diversity of play experiences and direct contact with nature has direct benefits for children's physical, mental and emotional health. Free play opportunities in natural settings offer possibilities for restoration, and hence, well-being. Collectively, the benefits fully support the outcomes established in Every Child Matters.
- Playful, experiential and interactive contact with nature in childhood is directly correlated with positive environmental sensibility and behaviour in later life.

The state of play: children's access to natural play spaces

- Extensive research indicates that opportunities for children to access and play freely in natural spaces are currently seriously compromised, due to a variety of interconnected factors.
- Adult influences and poor environmental quality negatively affect children's play behaviours and may distort the ways in which children instinctively interact with natural elements and environments.
- Given the significant benefits that arise from children's playful contact with natural environments, there may be discernible consequences for children's well-being from contemporary limitations and restrictions to outdoor play.

Supporting children's opportunities to play in natural spaces

- There are a number of existing 'compensatory' initiatives that seek to address the issue of children's access to natural play experiences – both as specific focused provision and at a more general level (i.e. dispersed outdoor play spaces).
- The development of local authority play strategies should clearly acknowledge the importance of children's natural play in natural space and identify appropriate responses to enhance children's play lives.
- Children's access to *everyday nature* needs to be protected and developed. This may comprise a mosaic of: designated nature sites, public green spaces, waste ground, school grounds and naturalistic playgrounds.

- Research principles and successful practice should be incorporated into the design of outdoor spaces that support children's natural play.
- The playwork sector working jointly with key partners has demonstrated a high degree of success across a range of projects supporting environmental play provision. Elements of good practice are emerging.
- There is a recognisable need to develop consistency in environmental play provision through: sustainable funding, training, networking and strategic support.

Opening clarifications

The theme of Playday 2006 was *Play, naturally* – chosen to represent the recognition that children have a natural drive to play and enjoy playing in natural environments. This review explores some of the research associated with this theme.

Intentionally the word 'nature', as the root of 'naturally', is used to represent two distinct meanings, which are indicated in dictionary definitions of the word. The first definition establishes the context for looking at nature and the natural environment:

● Nature – phenomena of the physical environment.

A second definition refers to:

● Nature – essential qualities, innate character.

This second definition of nature, that of biologically based inherent character, comprises two main relevant elements to this review:

1. Children's instinctive, irrepressible drive to play.
2. Children's inherent inclination to affiliate with nature.

What the theme suggests is a complex, reciprocal and mutually beneficial relationship between the playing child and the natural environment.

Overall aims

A diversity of environmental resources and access to play and exploration has been regarded as the two central criteria of a child friendly environment (Kytta, 2004). These two significant and inter-connected criteria form the underlying basis for this review. As such, the structure for the review is as follows:

Part 1 Having introduced the Playday theme this opening section will further elaborate on the meanings of 'play' and 'nature'.

Part 2 A consideration of children's biological drives: to play and to affiliate with nature.

Part 3 An exploration of the significance and value of children's playful encounters with natural spaces and elements.

Part 4 A discussion of contemporary changes in children's access to natural spaces for play.

Part 5 A review of the range of compensatory responses to create and enhance opportunities for children's play in natural environments.

The intention of this review is to give an indication of the connections across disciplines and open the possibility of reaffirming childhood as a period of natural emergence. Children, through their play, encounter their physical and social environments; they express their ideas, perceive possibilities and pose questions that invite a response. Through this dynamic, constantly changing process both player and environment have the potential to be transformed. The child, through playing in the world, is both being and becoming.

It is this process of 'playing naturally' that we consider through this review.

Defining nature

There has been a long history of identifying the unique relationship between humans and nature (particularly the relationship between children and nature). In developing this review, we may see that while 'environment' is relatively straightforward to define as the physical, biological and cultural conditions in which an organism lives, 'nature' is 'perhaps the most complex word in the language' (Williams, 1976; cited in Mergen, 2003). As a starting point, we may define nature as the natural physical world containing plants, animals and landscapes (including the inanimate elements that contribute to making up these landscapes), as in this dictionary definition:

> *All the animals, plants, rocks, etc. in the world and all the features, forces and processes that happen or exist independently of people, such as the weather, the sea, mountains, reproduction and growth.*
>
> (www.dictionary.cambridge.org)

In looking at the modern meaning of nature, Tuan (1978) notes that it is generally used to describe anything that has not been made by human beings. The 'natural environment' comprises all living and non-living things that occur naturally. In its purest sense, it is thus an environment that is not the result of human activity or intervention – and is often contrasted with the phrase 'the built environment'.

Tuan (1978) comments that for most of human history we have not made a distinction between the natural and the human designed environment. It was largely during the Industrial Revolution that distinction was attributed to the order and harmony represented through the natural world, and the chaos and disorder of human works. Over the past two hundred years or so, the industrialisation of much of the Western world, and increasingly so in non-Western countries, has given rise to a separation of the natural from the human designed. Currently we are witnessing such rapid technological change at a pace unprecedented in history (Gullone, 2000). Technology enables us to overcome the most inhospitable landscapes, to develop means of communication that are instant and global, to produce goods that were once thought to be the preserve of science fiction. These changes have drastically altered the face of the world.

More than 95 per cent of the earth is under direct human influence, while only 3 per cent of the surface is set aside as parks and protected areas (Baskin, 1997). Britain, as a small densely populated island, has little land area untouched by human activity except in inaccessible parts of Scotland and on the coast.

Thus, one may see there is a difficulty with the term 'natural environment'; nearly all environments in the UK have been directly or indirectly influenced by humans at some point in time. Many natural environments are the product of interaction between nature and humans, for example suburban gardens and highly cultivated farmlands (Tuan, 1978). Yet there still remain some areas that have not been influenced by human action, generally referred to as 'wilderness' spaces. For the purpose of this review, the term 'natural environment' may be seen on a continuum of human-environment influence, ranging from total human designed space to 'pure' wilderness (Carver et al., 2002); the phrase is dependent on context and degree rather than a set definition. Thus, in an urban context, a child may have daily access to a range of natural spaces with varying degrees of human design and modifications. The Wild About Play project provides a useful description of this diversity:

> *Wild spaces are green outdoor places where some areas are growing wild. They may be completely natural such as ancient woodland or be mixed in with artificial elements such as urban parks. Wild spaces come in many different shapes and sizes, and can be large or small, wet or dry, open or enclosed, near or far, tall or short, messy or tidy, green or brown … Wild spaces are: country lanes, hedgerows, woodland, city farms, grassland, beaches, heathland, gardens, rivers, shrubs, verges, ponds, fields, hills, parks, trees, farmland, sand dunes, village greens, muddy hollows.*
>
> (Wild About Play, 2004)

The term wild as used above brings a further dimension of natural environments that influence their utilisation by children: that wild spaces are perceived as relatively free from adult design and adult agendas (Maudsley, 2005; White and Stoeklin, 1998).

In searching for a definition that goes beyond the massively general and the restrictive, Louv (2005:9) proposes the use of the word 'nature' to represent:

> *… natural wildness: biodiversity, abundance – related loose parts in a backyard or a rugged mountain. Most of all, nature is reflected in our capacity for wonder.*

From the outset it should be recognised that animal and environment make an inseparable pair; 'each term implies the other' and no animal can exist without an environment (Gibson, 1986:8). In this mutual relationship, every animal is both a perceiver of the environment and a behaver in the environment. No individual organism can exist in isolation (Capra, 2003).

Defining play

Definitions of play, like attempts at defining nature, have been problematic (Power, 2000; Burghardt, 2005). As Sutton-Smith (1997) notes, we have all played, and may still play, and we know what playing feels like but when it comes to making theoretical statements about this we descend into 'silliness'. Fagen (1981) observes that play taunts us, as adults, with its inaccessibility. Bearing this in mind, this review adopts the most recent attempts to capture the essential qualities of playing as expressed through *Playwork Principles* (Play Wales, 2005):

> *All children and young people need to play. The impulse to play is innate. Play is a biological, psychological and social necessity, and is fundamental to the healthy development and well being of individuals and communities.*

This opening statement to the 'principles' clearly acknowledges the vital and 'natural' character of this behaviour, and further elaborates on this through the recognition that:

> *Play is a process that is freely chosen, personally directed and intrinsically motivated. That is, children and young people determine and control the content and intent of their play, by following their own instincts, ideas and interests, in their own way for their own reasons.*

Further support to these principles can be found in the *Charter for Children's Play* (Children's Play Council, 1998), *Best Play* (NPFA, Children's Play Council and PLAYLINK, 2000) and the assumptions and values of the National Occupational Standards for Playwork. However, we should recognise that any attempt to pin down children's play to a simple statement runs the risk of reducing this most complex form of behaviour to simplistic and potentially constraining perspectives.

Burghardt (2005) describes the numerous claims made for the benefits of play, citing over thirty functions attributed, including motor development, social and communicative skills, neural development, cognitive abilities and creativity. He comments on the importance of focusing on the value of the immediate benefits of play rather than longer term delayed benefits and suspects that 'this might be a more useful way to begin an approach to understanding the role of play in animals' lives' (Burghardt, 2005:117).

Best Play (NPFA, Children's Play Council and PLAYLINK, 2000) provides a useful introduction to key themes in the study of play and the benefits associated with playing. To gain a more detailed picture of the complexity of this behaviour one might start with *The*

Ambiguity of Play (Sutton-Smith, 1997), *The Playground as Therapeutic Space: Playwork as Healing* (Sturrock and Else, 1998), *Evolutionary Playwork* (Hughes, 2001) and *The Genesis of Animal Play* (Burghardt, 2005).

Approaches and influences

In addressing this topic, we may find that there are diverse disciplinary approaches that draw on, amongst others, biological, sociological and psychological perspectives. Interest in this theme relates to architects, planners, geographers, ecologists, politicians and so on. As Kahn (1999:1) explains, the topic involves understanding 'our biological roots … environmental behaviour, history, policy and science'.

The review is based on a wide-ranging search of materials that have addressed this issue and covers academic texts, newspaper and journal articles, promotional materials and research studies. It draws on materials from the UK, Europe, the US and other international sources, using university library databases and internet searches to identify significant and appropriate materials.

A rationale for undertaking this research can be found in Appendix 1.

While this review has looked at recent research into children's play in natural space, it should be acknowledged that there are some 'classic' works that have laid strong foundations for this area of study.

Children in place

Hart's (1979) detailed study of children's experience of place and Moore's (1986) exploration of children's playful use of their local environments stand as key texts and have had considerable impact on methods and concepts in studying children's relationship with the natural world. Ward's (1978, 1990) evocative studies of children in the city and the countryside also establish some central concerns and issues that retain currency and validity.

Tuan's (1974, 1978) exploration of the human attachment to place, referred to as 'topophilia' has again established an important framework for more recent approaches.

We may see that contemporary studies of children and their local spaces clearly acknowledge the significance of these key works.

Equally, Noren-Bjorn's (1982) critical evaluation of playgrounds in Sweden establishes some fundamental approaches to determining the play value of children's environments that are still highly relevant to contemporary approaches to developing compensatory play provision (Nebelong, 2002; Blinkert, 2004).

Studies of play

Bruner et al.'s (1976) collection of articles on play provides an introduction to the diversity of approaches to studying this 'antic topic', drawing on 'historical, literary, clinical, introspective, anthropological, sociological, linguistic, ethological and via controlled experimental methods of the behavioural sciences' (Bruner et al., 1976:13). The recognition of the centrality of play to evolution established through this collection has been further developed by a number of key works studying play in both humans and animals. Bringing this up-to-date, Sutton-Smith's (1997) analysis of play rhetoric covers the diverse ways of studying play through history and concludes with an influential chapter that has signposted further exploration of the evolutionary significance of play. Subsequent work by Sutton-Smith (1999, 2002, 2003) offers considerable promise for appreciating the complexity and vitality of the play process and we have highlighted some of these ideas at relevant stages in the review.

Equally, in looking at approaches to studying children's play, we recognise the significant contributions that Hughes and Sturrock and colleagues have made to developing an understanding of this form of behaviour and the implications for developing effective responses to supporting children's opportunity to play. Again, key themes from this body of work have been signposted in the opening stages of this review.

Environment and behaviour

Using Kahn and Kellert's (2002) collection as a starting point, we have been able to introduce some key concepts from the field of environmental psychology. Perhaps the most relevant aspects can be linked to Gibson's (1986) concept of affordances and Kaplan and Kaplan's (1989) work on place preference and restoration. Again, these ideas are presented in brief to establish the context for contemporary research.

Another significant theme developed through this account is the intimate connection between the child and its environment as eloquently expressed through the work of Edith Cobb (1977) in *The Ecology of Imagination in Childhood*. This work has again laid foundations in exploring the child's interdependence with their surroundings that resonates with the emerging field of environmental psychology and behaviour.

2

Children's natures

Children's biological drives

Hughes (2001:13) refers to drives as 'genetic rivers, whose primeval forces come from deep within us' and that play, as a drive exists to help children make sense of their immediate worlds. In this sense, play is seen as an 'instinct', and comparable to other biological drives that have evolved to maintain our survival – hunger, sexual activity, etc. They represent behaviour patterns that have adapted over the course of evolution to provide valuable mechanisms to support the biological needs of the organism (Bateson and Martin, 1999). As an evolved adaptation, they exist as modifications that make the organism better able to survive in a particular environment – 'better suited, that is, than if it lacked this crucial feature' (Bateson and Martin, 1999:5).

These behaviour patterns, while appearing as universal drives, are flexible in their expression; responsive to the immediate environmental conditions in which the individual develops. The growth and development of human beings is through interactions between evolved mechanisms and the environment and as such developmental patterns are not conceived as genetically predetermined 'but as a result of an evolved epigenetic[1] process that adapts human competencies to local conditions' (Blasi and Bjorklund, 2003:261). Bateson and Martin (1999) refer to this as the 'developmental kitchen' in which the raw ingredients of the many genetic and environmental influences are 'cooked' together through the biological and psychological processes of development; genes and environment provide the raw materials from which we construct ourselves (Rose, 2000). In this process, genes not only provide specific frames for a 'stable' lifeline, but also they provide for plasticity, the 'ability to respond appropriately to unpredictable environmental contingency, that is, to experience' (Rose, 1997:306).

Bogin suggests a possible adaptive value of the extended period of human childhood as 'a mechanism that allows for the more precise "tracking" of ecological conditions via developmental plasticity during the growing years' (Bogin, 1998:30). Given the complexity and variation of the 'human' environment, it is important that the young of the species have sufficient time and space to accommodate to the demands of that environment. The play drive or instinct, through the child's adaptive 'give and take' interactions with their environments, may be viewed as the primary mechanism for achieving this 'tracking'.

The play instinct

Prout (2005), citing the work of Rubenstein (2002), comments that play may be connected to the enhancement of social, physical and cognitive skills. This is not necessarily to prepare a child to become a better adult, but because the benefits of playing in the present moment help to make a better child.

Hughes (2001:xix), placing play firmly in an evolutionary frame, proposes that play enables children to fit themselves into their complex environments, to 'ground themselves physically and psychologically' in the here and now. At its most basic, we may see play is central to survival (Hughes, 2001). The use of the word

---

[1] Epigenesis – the emergence of new structures and functions during the course of development, through a bidirectional relation between all levels of biological and experiential factors … Functioning at one level of organisation influences functioning at adjacent levels, and therefore there should be substantial plasticity in development.

'survival' implies a sense of struggle, in which life hangs by a thread. But in play terms, survival represents a 'victory of life over death, a cause for celebration' (Chilton-Pearce, 1992:141).

This theme is explored by Damasio who notes that nature, not content with the 'blessings of mere survival', appears to have had a nice afterthought (Damasio, 2003:35). A biological need for maintaining life (homeostasis) does not simply require a 'neutral' state of balance between life and death; but rather the aim of homeostasis is to seek a better than neutral position, to place ourselves in favourable situations that enhance our lives, what we generally refer to as 'well-being'. The preferred state for survival would be through a 'positive' feeling – joy and pleasure – that demarks a smooth running of the system. Damasio (2003) sees the state of joy as defining a greater ease to act, and we may see play as children's wilful belief that they can act out their capacity for the future (Sutton-Smith, 1997, 1999). The opposite to this, as expressed through sadness and sorrow, is a disequilibrium in which the ease for action is reduced, leading to depression and psychological discord (Sutton-Smith, 1997; Damasio, 2003).

Recognising this, we may see play as a biological drive by which the child seeks to place themselves in a favourable position in their environments, as the earlier statements from the Playwork Principles indicate. Hughes (2001) emphasises the play drive may exist to guarantee that children engage with their world in such a way as to suit their abilities but also to maximise the opportunity for understanding how this environment works:

> *When we see a child playing with a flower, or in the dirt, or skipping or playing tag, we should remind ourselves that what we are looking at is the child-like result of a deep and irresistible urge to interact with and have knowledge of the world and everything in it.*
>
> (Hughes, 2001:13)

From this, we may deduce that where the environment is complex and offers limitless possibilities for engagement through a range of play mechanisms, provokes strong emotional responses from the child, and invites opportunities for exploration, risk and challenge then there will be the 'promise of more to come and do' (Cobb, 1977).

Noren-Bjorn (1982:188) illustrates this process:

> *Some children (four boys ranging in age from 5–10 years old) gathered around a puddle which had formed under the 'Shipwreck' equipment. They played with boats there and then one boy of about eight hit on the idea of getting some new-mown grass from a near-by slope. With the help of a younger*

boy he drove a big load of grass down to the puddle in a cart, emptied the grass into the water and stirred it around with long sticks. The children called it spinach. Gradually they began to lift up the slippery stuff and watch how the water ran off. Then they loaded the wet grass into the cart and took it over to the sand-pit, where they mixed it with sand and shaped it into a cake which they then proceeded to decorate with gravel and stones in a neat circle, finally adding sticks as candles. The boy who had started the whole thing then instructed the other boys to sing 'Happy Birthday' to him.

Play and brain development

Recent work by Sutton-Smith (1997, 1999, 2002, 2003) has explored the relationship between play, the environment and the function and development of the human brain. Collectively, these studies develop fascinating and complex themes that are beyond the scope of this review. However, we may highlight two relevant points from this research:

- Developing ideas from neuroscience, Sutton-Smith remarks on the enormous plasticity of the human brain in the early years, with the ability to respond to what happens in the external environment. Johnston (2004) comments that for the first decade and beyond the child's brain is under construction, and this is responsible for its capacity to be shaped or moulded by experience.
- Play is a child's way of creating an alternative or virtual reality, which helps to create the brief illusion that the limits of existence do not exist and therefore allows the child to play with possibilities. Sutton-Smith refers to this as a 'fabulating mind',[2] and suggests that through this process play promotes the realisation of brain potential. Yet this takes place without any 'real' commitment; what play offers is the exercising and saving of variability and flexibility that would not occur without play – an adaptive plasticity (Johnston, 2004).

Yet, as Sutton-Smith (1997) notes, to children play is about 'having fun', being outdoors and with friends, choosing, not working, pretending and fantasy, etc.

---

[2] Sutton-Smith refers to this as a brain that is always creating some kind of internal fiction, or 'is at play within itself'.

Play and emotions

Emotions are generated in the brain's limbic system. Essentially they are not feelings at all but a set of deep-rooted survival mechanisms that have evolved to turn us away from danger and propel us forward to things that may be of benefit (Carter, 1998). Our primary emotions are largely unconscious in their operation, particularly in the early years, but when we become conscious of these emotions, we may be said to have 'feelings' (Damasio, 1994, 2003).

On top of these primary emotions are 'newer', secondary emotions, arising from our evolutionary heritage of becoming social, thinking, reasoning creatures: embarrassment, pride, empathy, shame, guilt and envy, what Damasio (2003) refers to as 'social emotions'. These forms act as checks and balances against the primary emotions, and reduce the chances of trigger-like inappropriate emotional responses to the modern complexity of survival.

If the prime purpose is to maintain the optimum body state for survival, any experience is approached with this pre-set programme of preferences; they are integral to the process of reasoning and decision-making. Emotional responses allow us to categorise situations we encounter and connect these responses with appropriate thoughts and actions:

> Emotions and feelings have no crystal ball to see the future. Deployed in the right context, however, they become harbingers of what may be good or bad in the near or distant future.
> (Damasio, 2003:147)

Emotions, then, may be seen as the natural medium for the brain to evaluate the environment and respond accordingly. As Damasio (2003) highlights, the complexity of the human brain not only allows for an unconscious emotional response, but enables the individual to think about emotions, to name them as feelings and to map them for later use (what Damasio (1994) refers to as 'somatic markers'). Alongside this, humans can wilfully strive to manage and control emotions to a certain extent through a mediation process that enables situating oneself in circumstances favourable to survival.

The basis of the thinking behind Sutton-Smith's argument can be crudely summarised as:

- primary emotions are still needed in survival emergencies;
- because of this, primary emotions need to be exercised (which is what happens through play);
- at the same time, primary emotions need to be kept in check within the newer social emotions.

Sutton-Smith (2002, 2003) feels that the primary emotions are mediated through children's play by the secondary emotional controls that players bring into the play frame. Thus, in 'anger' play, instead of giving way to outright aggression and violence, the players display strategy and control. Where fear is the primary emotion, then this is counteracted through displays of courage and resilience, where sadness and loneliness underpins the play, children will develop ways of bonding and developing a group identity through the play frame. From this, Sutton-Smith proposes that it may be possible to connect certain types of children's play with this mediating process, e.g. play fighting and the balance between anger and contest; den making as a mediation of sadness and loneliness through developing shared spaces; fear mediated through deep play; disgust mediated through playful obscenities, etc.

Sutton-Smith (2002) suggests that this dynamic emotional interplay represents an 'endless evolutionary instigated drama', using the metaphor of the circus to illustrate how this works. In a circus, the animals symbolise the possibility of danger, the clowns symbolise the disruption of conventions, while the acrobats symbolise the disruption of physical safety. Yet all of this takes place in a circus tent, where it is known that nothing really dangerous or disruptive will happen[3] (Sutton-Smith, 2002:19). Yet as Sutton-Smith acknowledges, there will be times when the primary emotions seep into the play, when play fighting shifts into real fighting, when playful disgust teeters into real disgust and so on.

Perhaps the natural world provides a wonderful circus tent for children's play. There are amazing possibilities presented in a complex natural environment for a range of 'circus acts' – rich in environmental stimuli that are attractive to children and provoke a strong playful emotional reaction. Cobb (1977:48) sees a child's response to the natural world through play as a 'fingering over of the environment in sensory terms, a questioning of the power of materials as a preliminary to the creation of higher organisation of meaning'. Thus, a child may pick up a stick and draw pictures in the sand, creatively swirling the stick backwards and forwards, tracing over and through lines, wiping clear and starting again – a subtly shifting emotional state, working with environmental elements, giving meaning to the 'pictures' created through their actions and so on.

---

[3] But there may well be times when there are tragic accidents and things go wrong – and this adds to the suspense and mythology of the 'circus' – there is a remote possibility that the tightrope artist may fall from the wire.

The nature instinct

For most of our history, and indeed all of our pre history, we have had an intimate connection with nature and the natural world and from an evolutionary perspective it would be no surprise to still find echoes of this in our behaviour (Frumkin, 2001).

Our survival as human beings has required an ability to recognise dangers that the natural world presents and to take advantage of the many benefits that nature offers. Such a relationship would suggest that the natural environment is central to human evolution. Wilson's (1993) *Biophilia* hypothesis proposes that there is an innate emotional affiliation of human beings to other living organisms. Wilson's key points from the biophilia hypothesis indicate that this emotional affiliation is:

- Inherent and innate – the affinity for nature is biologically based.
- Part of our evolutionary heritage – Wilson (1993) maintains that our affiliation with nature has led to the acquisition of learning rules.
- Associated with genetic fitness – these learning rules enable survival.
- A contributory factor in achieving individual meaning.

It should be highlighted that this affiliation covers both positive and negative responses (what has often been referred to as biophilia and biophobia). Ulrich (1993) comments that having adverse reactions to natural features and creatures has had a high adaptive value, for example, fear of snakes, heights, caves, spiders, etc.

Evidence of this relationship and affinity could be evidenced through:

- The values we attribute to nature – we have a range of 'physical, emotional and intellectual expressions of the biophilic tendency to associate with nature' (Kellert, 1996).
- Aesthetics and habitat selection – preferences for sites that had some significant survival advantages from our past.
- A sense of well-being associated with contact with nature.
- Affiliation with animals – human contact with animals supports psychological health and well-being.
- The symbolic significance of nature – animals and, more broadly, nature play a prominent role in expression of language and thought.

Wilson's biophilia hypothesis attracts much criticism, principally around the genetic determinism of the argument and the failure to acknowledge the role of culture as a mediating process in human evolution. Kahn (1999) provides a useful summary of the key arguments made in favour and against biophilia, and concludes that the research 'speaks relatively strongly for the proposition that people have a need and propensity to affiliate with nature' (Kahn, 1999:43), but biophilia requires a framework that goes beyond evolutionary biology and takes into account development and culture. The introduction of a co-evolution stance, i.e. the interplay of genes, organism and environment, suggests a more fruitful approach to studying the human relationship with nature (Rose, 1997; Oyama, 2000; Lewontin, 2000; Prout, 2005). This approach allows a perspective that acknowledges the 'interpenetration' and plasticity of the relationship between organisms and the environment.

At its most simple (and most complex) every living human being and their environments are in a state of 'constant flux, at the same time both being and becoming' (Rose, 1997). Through a continuous process of give and take with the environment we seek to maintain a healthy balance. As we do this we are constantly changing the environment. What we have, through the period of childhood, are human beings who are biologically and socio-culturally designed to 'fit' themselves as *children* into the environment they encounter through the ability to 'self-organise' as a means of adapting to the complexity of a far-from stable environment (Lester, 2005).

This notion of a natural affinity has found many voices within the environmental literature, for example, Rachel Carson (1965), cited by Lear (1999:160) remarked:

> ... the affinity of the human spirit for the earth and its beauties is deeply and logically rooted ... a deeply seated response to the natural universe.

Similarly, Moore and Wong (1997) note that children have a natural affinity towards nature; children seem drawn towards earth, sand, water, trees and plants and small animals. Hart (1997) acknowledges the importance of children's innate sense of curiosity about the natural world and their struggle to work out their relationship to this as children's way of understanding about life and its meanings. This affiliation with nature requires the opportunity to have unmediated contact with the local environment.

Moore (1986:170) provides a wonderful illustration:

> 'We come here to look for squirrels,' Jenny said. 'In the spring we pick bluebells – not too many though. We chase around, but not hide-and-seek, in case one of us gets lost.' ... We followed a sunken path and wandered among the trees. A few large oaks rose above multitudes of multi-stemmed elderberry bushes spaced 8–10 feet apart. Bright sunlight shafted through the

*amber leaves and reflected of the golden carpet of those
already fallen. The effect was magical. Few words passed; they
didn't need to, the reality of the 'real forest' enveloped us so
strongly.*

In spite of the trend in urbanisation, children still had access to
their immediate environments and natural features – the streets,
green areas, playgrounds and parks, nearby wastelands, woods,
nature reserves all offered possibilities for exploration, expeditions
and playing with natural elements (White, 2004). It is perhaps in
more recent times that this has been more constrained through a
range of factors resulting in fewer opportunities for children to
access outdoor natural spaces (Valentine, 1997; Louv, 2005).

Moore's (1986) and Hart's (1979) classic studies of children's
experiences of their local environments portray children spending
time playing outdoors in natural sites and with natural elements.
Such a picture might be hard to envision today. The popular
impression in the UK of the contemporary landscape for children's
relationship with the outdoors would generally display a picture of
children's declining opportunity for unmediated outdoor play and
access to natural spaces (Valentine and McKendrick, 1997). The
prevailing 'culture of fear' (Furedi, 2002) instils in parents a sense
that the outside world is not safe; increasingly children's lives are
being highly organised and structured (Hocking and Thomas, 2003).

What we have at this point is recognition that children's play is
'natural'; children do not need to learn how to play, it is an integral
part of the innate character of a child. What we are also getting a
glimpse of at this stage is an appreciation of the complex
relationship between the child and its environment. Given what we
know about play and the associated benefits, children's natural play
is likely to thrive in spaces that support this drive, i.e. natural
spaces.

The complexity of the relationship between the child and nature

As previously indicated, the relationship between the child and their
immediate environments is highly complex. Aitken (2001) provides a
valuable introduction to the notion of the 'natural child' and the
influence of the Romantics in forming the modern themes of
childhood and nature. Aitken (2001) makes the point that
assumptions about the relationship between nature and childhood
are established and elaborated in scientific and popular discourses.
The influence of the Romantic movement, with notions of nature
and childhood as places and times of innocence, naivety and purity,

can still be found in 'a large swathe of contemporary Western thought and social science practice' (Aitken, 2001:33). Chawla (1994) comments on the 'misreading' of the Romantic poets and notes that alongside the expressions of wonder and beauty there was also a strong sense of the fear and dangers represented through natural forces; thus nature could be wonderfully calming and peaceful, yet also provide thunder and lightening; spaces of light and dark; soft dandelion seeds and thorns.

The influence of the 'natural child' discourse becomes apparent when we look at the romantic notions of the rural child as a representation of 'innocence, wildness, play, adventure, the companionship of other children, contact with nature ... healthiness, spatial freedom and freedom from adult surveillance' (Jones, 1997:166). Aitkin (2001) observes that such perspectives perhaps 'do violence' to the reality of children's everyday experiences.

Recent research into the lives of children living in rural areas has questioned much of this traditional perspective (Ward, 1990; Philo; 1992; Matthews et al., 2000a; Valentine, 1997; Mattson, 2002; Nairn et al., 2003; Giddings and Yarwood, 2005). These studies highlight the constant struggles of children and young people to achieve the 'rural dream'. Matthews et al. (2000a) in their study in Northamptonshire comment on the alienation, constant surveillance by adults, and dislocation that children and young people felt within the rural communities. Equally, parents in rural areas expressed similar levels of fears for their children as their urban equivalents (Mattson, 2002).

Smith and Barker's (2001) study of children's play in rural areas concluded that there were severe restrictions on children's independent mobility. Children's opportunities to play were limited through the geographical distance between friends, the privatisation of rural land and adult concerns over children's unsupervised use of public space (Giddings and Yarwood, 2005). Mattson (2002) notes from research in Sweden that children had less independent mobility than children living in towns.

We may also find other idealisations of relationships with the outdoors through perspectives on gender. A significant amount of research highlights the differing nature of boys' and girls' access to local space and their play patterns and behaviours within these areas. Hart (1979) and Moore (1986) commented on the different ranging limits of boys and girls within their detailed studies. Valentine (1997) noted that boys are more likely to be described as 'outdoor' children than girls and that more of boys' outdoor play will extend beyond the home site. Moore and Young (1978) commented that boys were allowed to negotiate ranging limits on the basis of the maxim 'boys will be boys', while girls were fixed in much more clearer and rigid sets of rules. Cunningham and Jones (1991) note the more frequent use of playgrounds by boys than girls accompanied by a wider ranging of boys to access play spaces. Karsten's (2003) research into children's use of playgrounds in Amsterdam reviews a range of studies that largely concur with this pattern but also comments on the ways in which the gendered space of playgrounds is contested by both girls and boys.

Yet this may be a changing trend and the gender gap may be narrowing (Valentine, 1997; O'Brien et al., 2000). Matthews et al. (2000b) in their study of the 'street'[4] as 'thirdspace' remarked on the sometimes mythic notion that boys play out while girls play indoors, at their friends' houses or in the mall where they 'play out their femininities'. Their study highlighted the value of the street as an important social venue for many young girls and that girls' use of these spaces rivalled that of the boys. Skelton's (2000) analysis of teenage girls in the Rhondda Valley also highlights a possible shift in the traditional patterns of gendered access to outdoor spaces.

Morris (2003) provides an invaluable review of black and ethnic minority relationship with public open spaces that again highlights the complexity of this issue, noting the insufficient attention that has been given to this area of research. The same criticism may also be addressed to issues of disability and inclusion and the representation of disabled children's interests in the planning and designing of public spaces (Dunn and Moore, 2005).

Thus, the romantic view of children and the natural world, the myths and narratives of children's playful encounter with nature need to be carefully balanced with an appreciation of our adult perception of children and childhood. Approaches to studying this relationship probably say more about the way that we view children rather than any reality of children's experiences (Aitken and Herman, 1997). Philo (1992:199) acknowledges that:

The meta-narratives which we conventionally relate about the social world inevitably steamroller over the more specific stories that 'other' peoples in 'other' places tell themselves when seeking to make sense of their specific and situated existences.

In placing children within these meta-narratives (or universal theoretical accounts) we reproduce a single category of 'child' that greatly oversimplifies the complexity of young people's lives and

---

4 In Matthews et al.'s (2000b:63) research, the term 'street' is used 'as a metaphor for all public outdoor places in which children are found, such as roads, cul-de-sacs, alleyways, walkways, shopping areas, car parks, vacant plots and derelict sites'.

reduces their experiences to fixed and predictable patterns. What is missing is the local and distinctive ways that children live in their childhood spaces (Philo, 1992).

O'Brien et al. (2000) highlight the importance of recognising that children's access to the outdoor world is a reflection of a complex web of connections including gender, ethnicity and family culture as well as local place characteristics. Accompanying these local 'conditions', O'Brien et al. recognise the influence of global conditions such as the nature of urban living and relationships between generations in the public and private sphere.

Thus, we may see children's environmental experience as a function of diversity and access; this will be influenced by a variety of social, cultural and physical factors. In *Childhood's Domain*, Moore (1986:36) used the metaphor of a tapestry to describe the intricate patterns woven by children's interactions with their spaces and each other:

> *Each child wove a pattern of personal play traces through the neighbourhood, laced together with the traces of other known and unknown players.*

This is a wonderfully evocative picture of the complexity and dynamics of children's encounters with their worlds: a cloth that contains some very detailed patterns, while other areas are largely avoided, where there is a constant shift in patterns according to seasons, changes in the landscape (both real and perceived) and the developing and severing of human relationships. As Moore explains, these are not tapestries that are fixed to museum walls, but are constantly evolving and new patterns emerging in response to experiences. This metaphor might also align with Prout's (2005) analysis of childhood, drawing on the work of Deleuze and Guattari (1988), to propose a landscape for children's lives that consists of two 'planes', a plane of organisation that seeks to place children under control, keep them safe, regulate and educate, while another plane sees children as plotting flights away from organisation, through contest, imagination, creativity, transformations or what may be generically referred to as 'play' (Lester, 2006).

Instinctive environmental exploration

When looking at the relationship between children and their local spaces, we may recognise that the child's primary mechanism for perceiving and behaving within their immediate environments is through play (Matthews, 1992). As Hughes (2001:1) comments, play is the 'psychic and behavioural equivalent of oxygen'. Bateson and Martin (1999) suggest that individuals:

... are active agents in their own development, seeking out and acquiring experiences that will change their future behaviour. Young animals and humans are equipped with developmental mechanisms that seem to have been designed specifically for this role. Collectively, the behaviour is called play.

(Bateson and Martin, 1999:196)

Hughes's (2002) exploration of play types and play mechanisms (Play Wales, 2002) provide useful approaches to considering the diversity and richness of children's play, to enable children to best fit their immediate human and physical environments.

Drawing on a wide range of play research, 'play types' refer to the diverse play behaviours that children exhibit as they encounter their immediate worlds. Hughes (2001, 2002) proposes that all these forms of play make a significant contribution to a child's health and well-being and collectively provide a child's repertoire of play behaviours.

While play types are largely descriptive of children's play behaviours, the notion of play mechanisms advances this concept into an appreciation of the mechanisms or modes of playing. Hughes (Play Wales, 2002) suggests that these mechanisms act as a filter for experiences – a concept that might align with Damasio's (1994) 'somatic marker' hypothesis. These mechanisms arise from the emotional response to an external stimulus, a response that is biologically framed and mediated through experience, into specific actions and behaviours designed to place the child in a favourable position with their environment.

Thus for example, a child in a natural setting may be deeply immersed in a microscopic element of the environment, lost in thought, or may be using the same environment as a source of physical challenge through climbing a tree. The environment also offers the potential for a range of other play modes – discovering insects under the bark of a tree, building a den, etc. Play Wales (2002) identifies twelve discrete play mechanisms and each of these clearly relates to modes of engagement with the environment.

Summary

It may be concluded that all children have biological predispositions that impel them to interact with the physical world around them. Children form relationships with nature instinctively and should be considered the 'natural' experts in play.

Given appropriate space and opportunity, children will enact the two basic drives explored in this section – to play and to affiliate with nature – in interactive, complex and individualistic ways.

- The drive for diverse and dynamic play propels the child to seek optimal play environments, which is arguably most completely fulfilled in natural settings. The natural world provides the major stimulus and the most significant context for experience (Moore, 1997). It is an ever changing and diverse scene, offering the widest range of possible interactions.
- The drive to affiliate with nature is activated and fulfilled through playful interactions with natural environments and elements, producing a range of responses and mental states in children.

3

The values and benefits of children's play in natural settings

Introduction

Tuan (1978) surmised that the relationship between children and the natural environment is complex and little understood, posing a number of key questions for research:

- How does such a setting compare in developmental effectiveness with the resources to be found in a human designed environment?
- In what ways can a natural setting affect the perceptual and conceptual development of the child?
- In what ways can a natural setting speed up the recovery of children from certain kinds of diseases?

During the past 30 years a substantial body of work has been developed to highlight the importance of the natural environment to human well-being and respond to the questions raised by Tuan and others (Wells and Evans, 2003; Morris, 2003).

Building on the questions above and on the information on children's natural drives presented in the previous section, this next stage of the review examines the values and benefits of play in natural settings through three key areas:

1. The utility of nature for optimising play experiences.
2. The responses and relationships with nature developed through play.
3. The capacity of nature for restoration of health and well-being.

However before exploring these themes it is necessary to frame them by considering children's favoured places for play.

Where children choose to play

Research with children continually highlights the importance children place on playing outdoors (Hart, 1979; Moore, 1986; Matthews, 1992; Rasmussen, 2004; Armitage, 2004; Burke, 2005). Survey statistics cited in Worpole (2003) reveal that '94 per cent of children would want to spend more time out of the house' and that '86 per cent of parents say that on a nice day their children would prefer to go to the park than watch TV'.

Millward and Wheway's (1997) study of children's play on housing estates found that children used a variety of spaces for meeting, being with friends and playing, not simply in adult designed sites. The study highlighted children's regular and favourite locations as open green space (56 per cent), street (26 per cent), gardens (23 per cent), play area (21 per cent), friend's home (19 per cent), trees (17 per cent), outside their house (16 per cent) and shops (14 per cent).

Thompson and Philo's (2004) study of where children play in Livingston, Scotland produced a mixture of 'adult spaces' along with the 'informal' spaces that children carve out for themselves. When asked what things they played in these places, children's favoured responses were: playing on bikes and rollerblading, playing in tree-houses and dens and playing in play parks. Thompson and Philo also highlight the importance children attributed to 'hanging about' with friends and 'having a laugh', chatting and generally being in places in which they could see and be seen.

Rasmussen and Smidt's (2003) study of children's perception and use of their environment provides an insight to the range of spaces and uses valued by children. Using photographic research with children to identify place preferences, the results show a 'chaotic multitude of places, items and persons' (Rasmussen and Smidt, 2003:89). The children's photographs showed:

- A range of places used by children in the neighbourhood, including playgrounds or nature playgrounds, slides, earth mounds, cabins, shacks and dens, swings in trees, old rowing boats.
- Alongside this, children identified a range of 'nature spots': trees, felled tree trunks, shrubs, stone walls, etc. It was noted that children viewed these places with an affordance of function and action – that they were valued because of what the spaces offered – trees were climbed, wild flowers picked and so on.
- Private buildings, places and areas, often home sites and gardens, streets, transitional niches between the home and the outside world such as back alleys, common greens around houses, etc.
- Movement – children included photographs of how they move around their immediate areas, for example on roller-skates, bicycles, home-made go-carts, alongside more formal transport such as cars and buses.
- Special persons – children took photographs of significant people who contributed to their place use and value.
- Animals – there is a considerable amount of research of the significance of this to children, in particular about how children develop environmental awareness and responsibility, and the therapeutic value of looking after animals in childhood (Myers and Saunders, 2002; Katcher, 2002; Frumkin, 2001).

Burke's (2005) study of children's play in east Leeds notes the large proportion of children's accounts of their play lives feature natural materials and environments. Her study revealed that 70 per cent of children's photographs were of outdoor spaces. As an example of this playful relationship with the outdoors, Burke explores the use of grass in children's play accounts:

> Young children appreciate grass, its aesthetic, its feel, smell, and function as a building material. They fight with grass and they mark out their boundaries with grass. Grass left after a mowing can transform a landscape into a new play opportunity.
>
> (Burke, 2005:46)

Collectively these studies demonstrate that children prefer to play outdoors, and in doing so seek out a range of different settings to fulfil their intentions. They also give a clear indication that children value playing in natural spaces; the content of these environments is likely to offer rich possibilities for active and creative engagement.

The utility of natural space for play

Natural playgrounds

As indicated above, natural environments have traditionally been a place for children's play (Fjortoft, 2004). Numerous studies have highlighted the rich potential in natural spaces to engage children across the full range of play types (Noren-Bjorn, 1982; Hughes, 2001; Korpela et al., 2002; Wells and Evans, 2003; Clements, 2004). Kellert (2002) considers the importance of the urge to master and control nature through risk-taking, adventures, control of the environment, independence and autonomy, den and fort making – coupled with risk avoidance, a fear of nature and a developing appreciation of the respect for the power of nature to destroy.

The natural environment also lends itself as a rich back drop to a child's imagination and fantasy, and Kellert cites the multitude of affective opportunities for engagement, surprise and discovery to be found in children's stories, myths and fables. This clearly has links with the taxonomy of play types developed by Hughes (2001, 2002).

Bixler et al. (2002) summarise the significant research around the area of children's play in natural sites, noting that:

- Exploration helps children develop wayfaring skills and provides time and space away from adults.
- Children develop positive attitudes towards the places they explore because these are places in which they are least inhibited.
- Wild areas provide a rich developmental landscape; natural environments are dynamic, complex and often disorderly: protruding rocks and tree roots, fallen trees, low-hanging branches, streams without bridges, and many geologic variations provide exciting psychomotor challenges.

The large number and variety of 'loose parts' (Nicholson, 1971) available in wildland environments along with the lack of close adult supervision provide greater potential for creative and constructive play than most built environments.

Hart's (1979) and Moore's (1986) classic studies of children's play patterns provide a wealth of detail on children playing out in their local environments. Using maps and drawings with children to identify their favourite paces, 96 per cent of the pictures were of outdoor places. From a child's perspective, the utility of nature is what the space offers to support their play. Children's perception and use of space may differ from adults' (Blinkert, 2004). Children are constantly asking the question what does this place have to offer to support play? This may be wonderfully illustrated by the following:

A girl throws a stone in the water. She listens to the plop and watches the rings forming. Another girl comes up and tries to hit a 'target' in the water. The girl begins to keep score of how many times they get a hit and to discuss what 'counts'.

(Noren Bjorn, 1982:29)

Affordances of natural spaces

The notion of 'affordance' features prominently in environmental research into relationships between humans and their environments. Originally proposed by Gibson (1986), Fjortoft (2004:23) explained affordances as the range of 'functions environmental objects can provide to an individual', for example, if a rock has a smooth, flat surface, it affords a person a place to sit; if a tree is well branched it affords the opportunity for a person to climb it. Fjortoft comments that this suggests an 'intertwined relationship between individuals and the environment and implies that people assess environmental properties in relation to themselves, not in relation to an objective standard'.

Kytta's (2002) analysis of the affordances of children's environments builds on the work of Gibson (1986) and Heft (1988). As Kytta (2002:109) summarises:

Affordances are the functionally significant properties of the environment that are perceived through the active detection of information. Affordances include properties from both the environment and the acting individual. Affordances are always unique and different for each individual and each specific group of people.

Chatterjee (2003) refers to the transactional nature of the concept of affordance, implying an active and reflective child who is as much influenced by the immediate environment as it is by her or him. This interplay might find a connection with Sturrock and Else (1998) 'ludic ecology' of the child. Sturrock and Else's (1998) exploration of the play cycle and play cues further develops the nature of the child's playful engagement with their immediate environment. Sturrock and Else propose that the child's internal psychic play frame communicates to their external environment through subtle cues. The cue is 'the signal for the world to engage with the child's developing sense of self and reality' (Sturrock and Else, 1998:19).

The continual interplay of call and response maintains this frame until such a time as the attraction of the environment wanes or the child's attention shifts to another area of focus.

Heft (1988) through research into observational studies of children's use of place produced an affordance taxonomy of children's environments. Significant features were (adapted from Kytta, 2002):

Environmental quality	Affordance
Flat, relatively smooth surfaces	Cycling, running, sports and games
Relatively smooth slopes	Rolling down on wheels
Graspable, detached objects	Throwing, digging, building, playing with animals
Attached objects	Jumping over, jumping up to and down from, balancing along
Non-rigid attached objects	Swinging and hanging, climbing up
Climbable features	Climbing, looking out from
Shelter	Hiding, being in secret places, quiet and solitude
Mouldable material	Building, shaping
Water	Swimming, fishing, general water play

Figure 3.1   Taxonomy of affordances

As well as these physical qualities associated with Heft's taxonomy, Kytta also adds another element, that of an affordance of 'sociality': that the space provided opportunity for social play, role playing, games of chase, opportunity to be loud and noisy, etc. Kytta's (2002, 2004) models provides a useful framework for exploring the relationship between children's mobility and the opportunity to actualise affordances (see Appendix 2 for an outline of this).

Frost (1992) develops the concept of 'playscape' in looking at children's play environments, arguing that natural features are an important quality of children's preferred play sites. Fjortoft and Sageie (2000) conclude their research into the natural environment as playground with further acknowledgement of the importance of the following features in providing high affordance for children:

● green structures (trees, bushes in diverse forms)
● loose parts
● diversity of topography (steep slopes, even ground, rough cliffs, etc.).

Natural diversity of environment and play experiences

Children's mastery and exploration of their environments is seen as a significant aspect of their play repertoires (Hughes, 2001). Exploratory play requires access to a variety of elements and different spaces with diverse surfaces and gradients. Hughes (2001) refers to mastery play as the child's attempts to master the elements and represents a child's way of engaging with the natural world.

Moore's (1986:55) study reveals a range of children's found and adapted spaces and children's ability to manipulate found objects in novel connections:

> 'We make streams in the sand when it rains and water comes down the hill,' the girls said. They got down on their hands and knees and embarked on a sequence of sand play. Within a few minutes they had laid out a network of 'roads' running around the humpy surface of the fine, hard-packed, sandy soil. Lesley was making a 'town with a motorway' with scattered groups of 'houses' (small mounds of dirt); Jill was working on a larger mound which she called a 'manor house'.

In her review of playgrounds in Sweden, Noren-Bjorn highlights the importance of play spaces to be as 'full of variety as nature itself' (Noren-Bjorn, 1982:187). This element of variety is shown in natural settings through ground cover (rocks, stones, sand, mud, water, grass, etc.), variety of spaces (secluded and open), loose parts that can be manipulated by children, and the possibility of 'chance' events.

Some more specific attributes of natural space for supporting children's play are explored in more detail below.

Loose parts

The affordance type in Figure 3.1 of 'graspable, detached objects' may be equated with the term 'loose parts' (Nicholson, 1971). Nicholson asserts that children love to engage with the physical environment and the features present in these spaces. It is now one of the most familiar approaches to exploring the relationship between play and environment, in a playwork context. The theory of 'loose parts' proposes that the possibilities for play, for interaction, exploration and discovery, creativity, etc. may be directly related to the number and the kinds of features in the environment. Nicholson suggests that the seashore represents an ideal play environment through its degree of disorder, the range of found components, variation of living and non-living objects, the constantly changing nature of the environment, etc.

Moore's (1986) interviews and observations with children highlight the way that certain terrains offer a rich potential for 'harvesting' – the collection of bits and pieces that could then be used in a variety of different ways, citing an example of 'loose parts' in which children navigated the steepest slope of a green site using milk crates which children had 'found' in local stores.

Trees and bushes

The affordance of natural loose parts is matched by fixed elements in natural spaces – notably trees and bushes – that are highly flexible and present a complexity of possibilities. Certainly the prevailing features in recollection of trees in adult memory of playing would support the importance of the tree being 'climbable', although there were instances where the base of the tree, or hollowed out trunks were cited as special places (Sobel, 1993). Nabhan and Trimble (1994:27) cite Ward's (1990) description of the value of trees:

> Trees can be climbed and hidden behind; they can become forts or bases; they become dens and little houses; they provide shelter, landmarks and privacy; fallen, they become part of an obstacle course; near them you find birds, little animals, conkers, fallen leaves, mud, fir cones and winged seeds; they provide a backdrop for every conceivable game of the imagination.

Similarly, Moore's (1986:167) accompanied journeys with children sometimes lead to significant tree sites, for example:

> Brian took me to a gnarled crab apple tree he and his friends liked to climb ... He showed me the remains of a camp they had built between the grounded branches. Another camp was located on the other side of the orchard, in a cosy 'found' space under the low-hanging branches of a yew tree: a special place by definition, since it was the only yew in the whole area. Alongside was an ancient apple tree with an upwardly curving trunk that Brian called his look-out tree, as he climbed to a horizontal fork, about seven feet of the ground.

Bingley and Milligan (2004) highlight the memories of the young people in their study group of playing in woodland spaces. The key theme to emerge from recollection of childhood play experiences is that interactions took the form of physical activity, particularly climbing trees and building dens.

Special places

A number of research studies note that there appears to be a universal childhood experience of making special places (Hart, 1979;

Moore, 1986; Dovey, 1990; Sobel, 1990, 1993; Nabhan and Trimble, 1994; Kylin, 2003). Kylin (2003) provides a useful review of the key themes in research on children's place making, both as physical objects located in physical spaces and places of special meaning. These studies link with Cobb's (1977) analysis of the critical stage of middle childhood as a time of bonding with and shaping the natural world. Echoing Hart's (1979) findings, Sobel explains that as the child moves from the home site they seek to create 'new homes, homes away from homes … a small world that they create from the raw materials of the natural world and their flexible imaginations' (Sobel, 1993:160). These creations of dens and shelters provide opportunities for children to bond with their natural worlds:

> *'Papa!' Laura cries. 'Come over and see the hideout we made beneath a tree over there. See if you can walk down the wash and find us. I bet you won't even be able to figure out where we are.'… I hear giggling coming from a concealed corner where a blackberry tree's canopy sweeps down to touch the ground. They have decorated a small opening with a wreath of wild flowers, and have made stools of pieces of wood found nearby… 'We've found the perfect place for eating cookies.'…*
>
> *Over time, I have come to realise that a few intimate places mean more to my children, and to others, than all the glorious panorama I could ever show them.*
>
> (Nabhan and Trimble, 1994:6)

Sobel (1990, 1993) outlines key qualities associated with the creation of these special places:

1. Special places are found and constructed by children on their own. They are unadulterated places that enable children to shape the place to their own needs without fear of adult reprobation, scrutiny or interference.
2. These places are essentially secret. They are only known to those who create them, and they need to remain unknown to others to retain their sense of 'specialness'. Children do not want to be found when inside these places and wish to remain unseen by others.
3. Special places are created by their owners. There is an adaptation process that claims this space, either through some physical adaptation, rites, or imaginative input.
4. Special places are safe for children. A feeling of calm and repose comes over children when they are in their special places. There is often a reflective or meditatively quiet aspect to being in their special places (see later in this review for a development of this key theme).

5. Special places are organised worlds. There is an intuitive process of arranging and fashioning the interior space, creating and constructing an ordered system.
6. Children's special places empower their builders.

Dovey (1990:16) includes an extract from an autobiographical account that is indicative of children's approach to the use of trees as a special place:

> *My favourite tree – I would spend many an evening just sitting there watching the view and the sunset. Here I would think and contemplate life. Lying comfortably on a branch, breathing the cool evening breeze and eating the fruit of the tree was the most heaven like experience I ever felt. I was at peace in this tree.*

Physical movement in natural spaces

Fjortoft's (2001, 2004) studies of children's play in outdoor natural environments notes that historically natural play spaces have been a key site for children's motor development but perhaps this is increasingly neglected. The research concludes physical play in a natural environment improved children's motor abilities and points to the natural playscape as an influential factor in children's motor development. Clements (2004) comments that between the ages of three and twelve a child's body experiences its greatest physical growth, as clearly evidenced by the child's 'urge to run, climb and jump in outdoor spaces' (Clements, 2004:69). This vigorous, playful movement enhances muscle growth, healthy growth of heart and lungs.

Veitch et al. (2006) note that time spent outdoors is one of the most consistent predictors of children's physical activity, and argue that among primary school children active free-play or unstructured activity that takes place outdoors in free-time may potentially be the major contributor to children's physical activity.

Moore and Wong (1997) observe how a diverse landscape encourages children's physical movement in all directions, describing how 'balancing, chasing, climbing, crawling, dodging, hanging, hopping, jumping, leaping, rocking, rolling, running, sliding, spinning, squirming, swinging, tumbling, twirling, twisting were all part of children's movements in a natural playground' (Moore and Wong, 1997:90).

The *Wild Adventure Space* review (OPENspace, 2006a) identifies the term 'green exercise' which highlights informal exercise in natural spaces and the interaction between activity and setting.

Children's independence

A child's ability to 'range', that is to move independently within their local environments, is considered to be vital to healthy growth and development (Moore, 1986; Gaster, 1991; Matthews, 1992; Huttenmoser, 1995; Sobel, 1997; Kytta, 2004). Children's ability to move in the home range is a 'transforming' mechanism through which children interact with and learn about their local environment, themselves, and others (Aitken, 1994; Matthews, 1992; Tandy, 1999; Spilsbury, 2005).

Rissotto and Tonucci (2002) maintain that children's independent mobility is central to the acquisition of spatial knowledge, particularly in situations where there is a desired purpose to moving in local environments. Within this context, children's environmental knowledge becomes an active problem solving process designed to enable children to carry out their preferred transactions. The quality of knowledge gained through this differs considerably from being accompanied by adults in the local environment.

Cornell et al. (2001), in their study of children's adventures and independent mobility, noted that when and as children had the opportunity to participate in self-directed adventurous journeying (i.e. where the outcomes from an unplanned journey were uncertain) they developed a series of strategies for coping with way finding and making sense of the space. Such strategies were complex and with use became increasingly more effective; and as they were context based, i.e. derived from direct experiences, they could not be formally taught.

Children's natural sense of wonder

Perhaps it is children's sense of wonder that presents the conceptual link between their exploitation of natural spaces to optimise playful instincts and the development of natural attachments to nature through play.

A significant contribution can be found through the work of Edith Cobb (1977) whose study provides a complex exploration of the child's relationship with nature and suggests that direct contact with the natural world supports a child's capacity for creativity, beauty and identity. Cohen (1996) makes similar claims when exploring children's acquisition of an aesthetic appreciation of nature; that through contact with their immediate environments children acquire a sense of what their spaces 'look like' and 'feel like' and how it affects and is affected by them. Citing the work of Hodgson (1988), Cohen maintains that through sensory immersion in nature, children develop an aesthetic appreciation of patterns, colours and designs.

Cobb's review of approaches to understanding children and nature highlights the gulf between scientific approaches of conquest and ecological perspectives in which primacy is given to the beauty of the child's thoughts and play without muddying the waters through adult speculations and interpretations of what this might mean.

Cobb's ecological perspective allows us to see the child as a part of an interdependent system; the child acts with and is acted upon within their immediate environments; 'plants, animals and humans must now be thought of as living in ecosystems, in a web of related, interacting, dynamic energy systems' (Cobb, 1977:24). This mutuality, what Cobb refers to as the adaptive give and take, represents the ecology of the child.

The period of childhood is a time when the child is engaged in a continuous response to the external world, giving rise to 'novelty of pattern and form' from the information presented, an intuitive sense of wonder, which is a prerogative of childhood. As Cobb explains:

> *Wonder is, first of all, a response to the novelty of experience. Wonder is itself a kind of expectancy of fulfilment. The child's sense of wonder, displayed as surprise and joy, is aroused as a response to the mystery of some external stimulus that promises 'more to come' or better still 'more to do' – the power of perceptual participation in the known and the unknown.*
> (Cobb, 1977:28)

Cobb's account of the child's 'patterning' of their environments through their 'fingering over of the world' (play), their creation of meanings from their sensory engagement with the natural world, their growing sense of self and identity, of continuity and discontinuity and their understanding and use of language finds much in common with a development systems approach (Oyama, 2000).

Children's responses to nature through play

Aesthetic values

The aesthetic value or perspective emphasises a primarily emotional response of intense pleasure at the beauty of nature (Kahn, 1999). Cohen (1994) cites the work of Adams (1991) and the importance of contact with nature for developing aesthetic values. Cohen's review of research suggests that through direct contact, children develop a sense of 'rootedness' and acquire a sense of environmental heritage.

Kaplan (1992) suggests that preferences are made largely through an affective response to the surroundings; surroundings evoke strong feelings. This 'reading' of the potential of the environment is an ongoing process leading to the possibility of further exploration and ranging, requiring further analysis and information collecting. Orians and Heerwagen (1992) emphasize that this model is a complex and dynamic process. All stages are continuous and simultaneously give rise to changes in feelings, behaviours and actions. This aesthetic appreciation of the potential of an environment to support action connects with the notion of 'affordance' previously outlined – what does this space afford for my own needs at this particular time?

Environmental preferences

Gullone (2000) states that certain landscape features that we find aesthetically pleasing today may have an affinity with those that enhanced the survival of the species – for example, bodies of water, plants and animals, higher areas, trees with low trunks, trees with high canopies (Appleton, 1975; Ulrich, 1993; Kahn, 1999; Wilson, 1984). Wilson (1984) notes that a crucial step in the lives of most organisms is the selection of a habitat that will support their survival. If the organism gets to the right place, everything else is likely to be easier. At this point, it is possible to introduce a suggestion that play might be a primary mechanism for children's niche construction; a process for placing themselves in their environments on their terms as children, not as potential adults (Lester, 2006).

Orians and Heerwagen (1992, 2002) explore how aesthetic reactions to landscape may have arisen from an evolved psychology that enabled our ancestors to make better decisions about where to move and settle. From an evolutionary perspective, it is reasonable to anticipate that humans will demonstrate preferences for environments that are beneficial, therapeutic or healthful (Wells and Evans, 2003). Kaplan and Kaplan (1989) also comment on the significance of an aesthetic appreciation to environment preferences. They note that perception is an important survival mechanism, being adaptive to perceive danger. But on its own this is not sufficient:

> *If the information an organism acquires through the power of perception is to aid in its survival, it is essential that it not only perceives what is safe, but also prefers it.*
> (Kaplan and Kaplan, 1989:41)

Qualities of preferred spaces

Kaplan and Kaplan (1989) identify further components in developing environmental preference:

1. Complexity – Kaplan and Kaplan suggest that people prefer the mid-range of complexity, avoiding extremes of low and high complexity, where there is richness, intricacy and diversity. The potential for exploration is enhanced in environments of favourable complexity.
2. Coherence – a factor that provides a sense of order and directs attention. 'Coherence is enhanced by anything that helps organise the patterns of brightness, size, texture in the scene into a few major units' (Kaplan and Kaplan, 1989:54). Coherence requires little inference, it is readily apparent, but having order does not necessarily reduce the complexity of an environment.
3. Legibility – a legible space is one that is easy to understand and remember, easy to find one's way through and to find a way back to the starting point.
4. Mystery – a promise of things to come and things to do: 'Something in the setting draws one in, encourages one to enter and to venture forth' (Kaplan and Kaplan, 1989:55). It provides a sense of anticipation, citing Cullen's (1961:51) discussion of mystery as 'those aspects of here and there in which the here is known but the beyond is unknown'.

An appreciation of an initial aesthetic response as a drive to place oneself in a desirable position leads to Orians and Heerwagen's (1992) application of 'prospect-refuge' theory; that people will prefer places that allow them to see without being seen. Alongside this, where there is a perceived hazard, the desire for refuge should be heightened. The authors emphasise the importance of small-scale urban natural spaces in meeting most of the above considerations. Also the current focus for all-round visual access in public spaces (as evidenced through the removal of bushes and shrubs on safety grounds) is likely to reduce or remove any visual appeal or mystery within spaces.

Children's attraction to natural spaces

Kirby's (1989) research into pre-schoolers' play in a USA playground, cited in Nabhan and Trimble (1994), found that they spent over half their time in three small refuges. A quarter of their time was spent in a found den under bushes and trees, where they played their dramatic, fantasy games. When not in these refuges, they spent another quarter of their time on two elevated decks used as 'lookout' posts:

When Kirby asked one four year old why he preferred such hiding spots with small openings, he replied, 'Because I would need to see if you were coming'. Probed further about why it was important to have a peephole for seeing out from his protected place, the boy responded matter-of-factly, 'Because there might be wolves out there.'

(Nabhan and Trimble, 1994:8)

In considering the attraction of natural space, Kaplan (1995) proposes that nature offers a rich combination of place preference components. The natural environment provides a space that is aesthetically and qualitatively different from the human built world (Sebba, 1991) and offers diversity, legibility and complexity in a continually changing space (seasons, light, growth, etc.).

Hart's (1979) detailed study of children's feelings about place discovered that natural settings (lakes, brooks and small frog ponds, woods sand piles, hiding and look-out places) were highly valued. Children in the study also expressed place fears that resembled the 'archetypal scary places of children's literature: abandoned buildings, woods, attics, cellars, and bedrooms and garages at night' (Hart, 1979:344). Yet while the darkness and solitary nature of these places are fear provoking, they were also perceived as favourable places for play.

Bachelard (1969) tellingly refers to children's 'side-hill', as a place of refuge away from the adult controlled and organised spaces. The 'side hill' represents a site of boredom, reverie and childhood imaginings that are remote from adult given ways of seeing and being and enable children to see the world from their own perspective.

Chawla's (2002) collection of studies about children and their local communities around the world identified a number of commonalities related to children's happiness with the places they inhabit:

- safety and freedom of movement
- social integration
- a variety of interesting activity settings
- peer gathering places
- cohesive community identity
- green space.

Developing a sense of place

Children's places are not simply a physical space of size and landmarks, but places where they carry out environmental transactions (Matthews, 1992); they are multi-layered and multi-faceted (Garbarino, 1985); what Hart (1979) refers to as 'phenomenal landscapes'. Tuan (1974) explores how attitudes and beliefs about our environments are formed and sustained, using the phrase 'topophilia' to describe the 'affective bond between people and place or setting' (1974:4). 'Topophilia' expresses a complex relationship that may arise from an aesthetic appreciation of the space, or from tactile experiences through playing with natural elements. More permanent and less easy to express are the feelings that one has toward a place because it is home, the locus of memories, and a place where one 'lives'.

The study of the human relationship to place and place attachment is wide ranging (Relph, 1976; Altman and Low, 1992; Massey, 1994; Hay, 1998; Gustafson, 2001; Derr, 2002; Manzo, 2003). Guiliani and Feldman (1993) in their review of place attachment literature note that there is a common appreciation of the positive value of an emotional/affective bond with place. Wallenius (1999) considers the environment to be a central part of life, identity and ability to maintain a sense of well-being. Gustafson (2001) comments on the significance of environment self-relationship in which people, through shaping the physical environment (building, cultivating, etc.) and being able to perform certain activities (in the child's case, play) perceive their environments as meaningful. The creation of a sense of place 'is important in maintaining the quality of the environment as well as the integrity of human life within it' (Derr, 2002:126).

Manzo's (2003) study demonstrates how affective relationships to place encompass a broad range of physical settings and emotions; are ever changing and dynamic; exists at both conscious and unconscious levels and are intimately related to the larger socio-political climate.

Derr's (2002) research into children's sense of place further explores the intricacies of the connections that children establish with their environments. Derr notes 'multiple scales' of experiences that influence place attachments:

- Child-scale experiences – the everyday play activities and lives of children.
- Family-scale experiences – provides the historical and cultural context for experiences.
- Community level experiences – where broad cultural values and place relations are shaped.

Derr (2002) acknowledges that each is important in 'what children learn from it, in what benefits they gain, and ultimately the type and extent of connections they will hold for place and nature'.

Through composition analysis, mapping and semi-structured interviews with children aged between 6 and 11, Derr (2002:126) identified four broad themes related to the children's experience of a sense of place (Figure 3.2).

Theme	Description
Four wheelers, ramps and rites of passage	Children learn through adventure, risk-taking, exploration and self-created rites of passage. Experiential needs greater than place attachments.
The fort makers	Children experience imagination, escape, safety and creativity through active place making and place attachment. Place and place making integral to the experience.
Learning care	Children learn nurturance, companionship, respect, awe from animals, ethnobotany, gardening and place. Elements of nature help children to model care for larger scale.
The web	Experience of a cultural place, reasons to stay, reasons to go, rootedness vs transience. Context for experience influences the meanings children attach to place.

Figure 3.2   Derr's themes of place relationships (Derr, 2002:126)

Chatterjee (2005:2) poses the question 'is it possible for children to develop "friendly" relationships with the physical environment?' and through a synthesis of environmental psychology, environment-behaviour and children's geographies outlines a conceptual framework for identifying key elements in a child's friendship with place (see Appendix 3 for an outline of this model).

The 'spiritual' connection between children and nature

Sheldrake (2001) notes that we need to think of what is unique and special about our surroundings so that we can get a better understanding of ourselves and our relationship to others and maintains that for this reason the human sense of space becomes a spiritual issue. Taylor's (2001) review of nature-based spirituality expresses the notion of spirituality as a way of describing what 'moves people most deeply'.

Spirituality has become a term that describes our deep relationship with the world 'with ideas of wholeness, creativity, and interdependence, with the interfusion of the spiritual, the aesthetic and the moral' (King, 1996:345).

Naess (1973) coined the term 'deep ecology' to express the idea that nature has intrinsic value and to criticise anthropocentric, 'shallow' environmentalism, for its instrumental view towards nature. Extending this, Capra (1997:7) notes that the human spirit can be understood as a mode of 'consciousness in which the individual feels a sense of belonging, of connectedness to the cosmos as a whole'. Shultz et al. (2004) highlight the significance of 'connectedness', the degree to which one associates with nature, as directly related to the types of attitudes one develops to the natural world.

Hart maintains that adults should 'feed' children's natural desire to contact nature with free access over an extended time period 'for it is only by intimately knowing the wonder of nature's complexity in a particular place that one can fully appreciate the immense beauty of the planet as a whole' (Hart, 1997:19).

Conway et al. (2004:4) notes that:

> *There are profound connections between the playing child in the microcosm of the playspace and in the wider macrocosm of environmental awareness. This ecological perspective can only be arrived at and more crucially, sustained by means of playing. The urge to sustain life can only be understood through the deep grammar of sustained playing.*

Ota et al. (1997) describe children's search for meaning in their playgrounds and cite comments made by a 12-year-old, writing about a miniature garden he had made:

> *... there is part of me which says my garden is wrong although I like it to have infinite beauty it cannot because there is a rule and that is the rule of nature that says everything must die and that rule can't be broken so the flowers must and will wither and the bark must crumble plus if you have something of great beauty that has never lived then it will never wither or crumble but when you have so much of it, it becomes normal and therefore loses its beauty and specialness.*
>
> (Ota et al., 1997:23)

Spots in time

Taking the themes developed by Cobb (1977), Chawla (1990) highlights the importance of 'ecstatic' memories of childhood places to adult health and renewal. Connecting with the ideas of Sobel (1990) and Dovey (1990), Chawla's analysis of autobiographical accounts of significant childhood places identifies a number of qualities associated with these powerful memories: places were usually outdoors, lent themselves to multi-sensory discovery, and were always marked by the 'psychological freedom of undisturbed encounter' (Chawla, 1990:21). In addition, there was a sense of 'mutual appropriation' in ecstatic places; the child belonged to the space because, in some way, the space belonged to the child. Chawla highlights the importance of such memories to producing meaningful images, a sense of calm and tranquillity, a sense of integration with nature and a creative disposition. This concurs with Sebba's (1991) consideration of the role of immersion in natural surroundings in a deep and direct manner to the creation of positive adult memories.

Schroeder and Lewis (1991), using Kaplan and Kaplan's (1989) concepts of restoration, note the importance of positive memories for developing and maintaining deep-seated, emotional or spiritual connections with nature, with associated benefits for mental health.

Developing positive attitudes to nature

The connection between playful contact with nature and environmental learning and awareness is addressed in a number of significant studies. Chipeniuk's (1995) study of the 'foraging' behaviour of children notes that children who reported foraging for the greatest breadth of naturally found elements demonstrated a higher degree of knowledge of biodiversity and environmental awareness as adults.

Bixler et al. (2002), in their study of children's play in wildness areas, reports that respondents who played in wild environments had more positive perceptions of natural environments, outdoor recreation activities, and future indoor or outdoor occupational environments. The study extends issues raised by Chawla (1992, 1994) in her analysis of adult recollections of preferred play sites as children and their adult attitudes to the environment.

Recent work by Schultz et al. (2004) highlights how individual concerns about nature are related to the extent to which people believe they are a part of nature. In their analysis of recent research, the authors consider levels of relationship that may exist among individuals, from a person who sees themselves as separate from nature to the individual who believes that they are connected to nature at all levels and in all forms. The study refers to this sense of connectedness as often being an implicit or 'primitive'; that is, this is often not a conscious, thought out position and concludes that the degree to which an individual associates him or herself with nature is directly related to the types of attitudes the s/he develops. In essence, individuals who associate themselves with the natural environment tend to hold broader sets of concerns for environmental issues.

Wells and Lekies (2006) examination of the connections between childhood involvement with the natural environment and adult environmentalism largely confirms the findings of Bixler et al. (2002). Their conclusions to the study highlight the significance of playful, unmediated contact with nature before the age of 11 as a 'particularly potent pathway towards shaping both environmental attitudes and behaviours in adulthood' (Wells and Lekies, 2006:13). Lohr and Pearson-Mims (2005) assert that a child's contact with nature, through tending gardens, playing in parks, being in spaces with trees and regular daily contact with a changing natural space are significant predictors of positive adult beliefs about the benefits of nature.

Collectively, these studies indicate that children's playtime in natural environments make a positive contribution to adult attitudes, knowledge and behaviour towards the environment (Wells and Lekies, 2006). Moore and Cosco (2000) assert that the biological health of the planet and human beings are interdependent.

Natural connections

Chawla (2002), adopting Gebser's (1985) philosophical concept of consciousness, suggests that direct experiences with nature help children form an 'integrated consciousness', a healthy mental and physical state that expresses a connection with the natural world. This analysis draws together much of the work outlined in previous sections:

- Archaic identity – a sense of immersion and assimilation of the surrounding world, positive place attachments.
- Magic relationships – echoing the work of Cobb and a child's sense of wonder and amazement, the creative forces of nature that produce ecstatic memories.
- Mythic places – the world half created and the world half received marks a period of investing places with dramatic meanings.

Collectively, these forms of consciousness suggest finding time for escape and restoration in natural surroundings, playing with natural elements, creating special places, realising the potential affordances that nature offers through play and developing an attachment and affiliation with such spaces.

Olds (2001) considers that with age adults lose an appreciation of the subtleties of the environment, while children are exquisitely sensitive to all qualitative aspects. Such sentiments would find a voice with the work of Cobb (1977) and the child's sense of wonder and sensuous engagement with their worlds. Through their playful encounter with the natural world children gain both a sense of continuity (a oneness and connection with the natural order) and discontinuity (a recognition of their own bounded-ness and separation of self vital to developing identity).

The value of natural space for restoration and well-being

There is good scientific evidence that contact with nature can improve mental health and can help in the restoration on psychological well-being (Douglas, 2005). During the past thirty years numerous studies have illustrated the role of natural environments in supporting well-being (Wells and Evans, 2003).

Ulrich's (1984, 1993) extensive research on the value of views of nature, as an initial aesthetic response, indicates a positive correlation with enhanced emotional well-being and stress reduction.

Attention Restoration Theory

Perhaps the most significant work on the role of nature in supporting restoration can be found in the development of Attention Restoration Theory (ART) developed over time by Kaplan and Kaplan (1989, 1995, 2001, 2002). Kaplan and Kaplan (1989) outline the notion of 'restorative environments' to cope with mental fatigue. The authors define 'mental fatigue' as an 'overworked capacity for mental attention'. Such restorative environments would contain a number of key qualities:

- Opportunity for escape – a need to get away from what is ordinarily present and generally not preferred. Kaplan (1995:173) recognised that being away required a 'conceptual rather than a physical transformation'. Simply taking your problems to another place is unlikely to be restorative.
- Opportunity for another context – a new extent of space, either physically of perceptually, imagined as well as real. Kaplan (1995:173) explains that the place must be 'rich enough and coherent enough so that it constitutes a whole other world'.
- Fascination – a source of interest.
- Action and compatibility. There should be a match between the environment and one's purposes and interests.

Kaplan and Kaplan (1989) argue that, while a wide variety of environments would offer the above qualities in various combinations, the notion of experiencing nature figured most prominently in research studies. They concluded that the natural environment appears to have a special position in meeting these requirements. While the authors focused on the significance of 'wilderness' space, they acknowledge that 'nearby natural settings' serve a similar (if somewhat less intensive) purpose.

More recent work by Kaplan (2001) extends this concept of nature and restoration. Citing the work of James (1892), Kaplan distinguishes between deliberate 'directed attention' and 'fascination'. Directed attention necessitates effort to get through a boring or difficult task and because it takes effort, is susceptible to fatigue. Directed attention contrasts with fascination, a state of attention that is effortless, that arises from excitement and interest and is less susceptible to tiredness.

The directed attention process, through the effort required to maintain the attention, can be seen to be a fragile process and subject to fatigue with possible consequences of:

- Readily distracted – maintaining focus is difficult.
- Planning impairment – difficult to plan and foresee possible futures. May have difficulty sticking to plans.
- An inclination to be impulsive – little patience or capacity for delay – act on the first thing that comes to mind.
- Inclination to be irritable.

While temporary states of directed attention fatigue can be managed, where it is pervasive and long-term, there are obvious detrimental and harmful consequences. Kaplan (2002:6) suggests that an antidote to directed attention fatigue might be through shifting focus to a more desirable form of attention, namely fascination. 'Fascination provides a way for directed attention to rest … since fascination itself is resistant to fatigue and takes no effort, being in its presence permits DAF[5] to recover' (Kaplan, 2002:6).

Fascination has two forms, content (the place of fascination) and process (the experience of fascination). These forms can be linked to the qualities of preferred surroundings previously outlined (complexity, legibility, coherence and mystery). Following this, we may see children's play as a 'fascinating' process in which children actively seek out environmental stimuli to escape, in spaces that provide a rich source of complexity, coherence and mystery.

---

[5] Direct Attention Fatigue

Support for Attention Restoration Theory

Kaplan's proposals have found support from a number of perspectives. Hartig et al.'s (1991) study into the restorative effects of natural spaces suggests that people experience gains in self-esteem and competence through their contact with nature. Kuo and Sullivan (2001) highlight the role of natural space in overcoming economic and social disadvantage, aggression and violence, etc. Their study of the relationship between mental fatigue and acts of aggression in inner-city housing estates concludes that residents living in more barren environments had higher levels of aggression than those living in places where there was regular access to natural features.

Taylor et al. (2001) describe the potential benefits of playful contact with natural space for children with Attention Deficit Disorder (ADD). The research asserts that, compared with the after-effects of play in paved outdoor areas, children diagnosed with ADD when playing in green spaces are far more likely to be able to focus, concentrate and pay attention following the experience. The findings to their study indicate:

> Not only … a strong nature–attention relationship, it also suggests a direction to that relationship. Because this study specifically focuses on attentional functioning after activities, it seems more plausible that participation in green activities causes improved attentional functioning than that improved attentional functioning causes participation in green activities.
> (Taylor et al., 2001:71)

While the study focuses on children with ADD, the authors feel that, as a general principle, the nature–attention relationship would apply to all children. They suggest that all children's attentional functioning might benefit from incorporating vegetation into places where children live and play. This would give further support to the considerable literature on the benefits of nature and encounter with the natural world for children.

Wells' (2000) study of the effects of 'greenness' on children's cognitive functioning indicates that the effects of natural elements within children's immediate home sites had a profound impact on children's ability to maintain directed attention. Wells comments on the significance of this to children's well-being through recognising that children's fascination and attraction to natural spaces is likely to be continually renewed and not subject to become boring. Further research by Wells and Evans (2003) suggests that levels of nearby nature moderate the impact of stress on the psychological well-being of children.

Place and well-being

The work of Korpela and Hartig (1996) extends the notion of restoration through encounter with natural space to a connection with the development of place identity. Children may become attached to certain places because it supports self-regulation; children and young people will seek out and visit favourite places to relax, calm down and clear their minds after threatening or emotionally negative events. Korpela et al. (2002:387) present the role of self-regulation as a process of maintaining balance between pleasant and unpleasant emotions and a key part of this process is through environmental strategies. This connects with Sobel's (1993) study of children's place making and Dovey's (1990) review of adult memories of their special childhood places.

Restoration of mental health

Access to local environments for play will also have an impact on children's mental health and well-being. The Mental Health Foundation (1999:6), in defining a child's mental health, highlights a number of contributory abilities among which were the ability to:

- Use and enjoy solitude.
- Initiate, develop and sustain mutually satisfying personal relationships.
- Play and learn.
- Resolve problems and setbacks and learn from them.

The report outlines factors that contribute to a climate for promoting children's mental health, including unsupervised play as a medium for risk-taking and decision-making leading to increased resilience and self-confidence.

Similarly, research by Bingley and Milligan (2004) highlights the benefits that young people gain from having access to natural woodland space. The study, conducted with seventeen 16- to 21-year-olds, looks at the relationship between their childhood play spaces and current strategies for coping with stress and notes that childhood play space experience appears to have a direct relationship with whether an individual chooses, for example, to go into woodland areas or simply visit a park or some other local 'natural' environment. The young people from this study recounted a range of play experiences, but the 'key influence on long-term confidence to walk in woodland, appeared to be the degree to which they had been able to experience unstructured play in woodland areas with little or limited adult supervision' (Bingley and Milligan, 2004:32).

Bingley and Milligan (2004:68) conclude that a woodland space was considered to be of great benefit for mental health and well-being for many of the study group. Where nearby woods are accessible it provides a space away from the usual places:

> *An important element of woodland is the fact it offers contact with a non-human and diverse environment. Some of these aspects are reported to be particularly relaxing, notably the diverse sensory experience of colours, scents, touch and sounds, which arise from wildlife, plants and trees. There was a sense of freedom in getting away from the 'stressful' situation at home, school or in a relationship. In other words there was relief in escaping from a human-orientated space infused with human-generated stress into this non-human dominated space. The aim was to be free, temporarily, from obvious human reminders of the source of the upset and distress.*

Summary

There is abundant and wide-ranging research that highlights the significance of children's play in natural space. Natural environments provide rich settings to support children's play drives, affording a diversity of possibilities for play behaviours. Such play experiences fulfil their biological potential for connection and affiliation with the natural world.

We have identified research that supports the importance of children's play in natural space and associated benefits to health and well-being. We may see that these benefits are for children in the here and now, enabling children to find their place within their local worlds. Such contact also enhances cognitive, physical and affective development in children, and may profoundly influence future individual and societal relationships with the natural world.

Kellert (1996, 2002) proposes nine values that may be used to describe the children's relationship with the natural world. A summary of these values can be found in Appendix 4.

Every Child Matters

Collectively the research indicates the overwhelming importance of children accessing natural space for play. It is worth indicating the possible connections between children's play in natural spaces and the five outcomes of Every Child Matters (ECM).

ECM outcome	Play, naturally – research evidence
Being healthy	Most research about children's play comments on the contribution that play makes to children's health, well-being and development (Best Play, 2000). Natural spaces offer optimal opportunities for physical motor development and associated health benefits from sustained activity (Moore, 1986, 1989; Moore and Wong, 1997; Fjortoft and Sageie, 2000; Fjortoft, 2001; Ebberling et al., 2002; Mackett and Paskins, 2004).

Playing out in natural space also contributes to positive mental health (Mental Health Foundation, 1999; Douglas, 2005).

The diversity and potential affordance of natural spaces supports wide-ranging play behaviours and mechanisms that offer children the opportunity for emotionally mediated play experiences (Sutton-Smith, 2003).

A child's play in green space, as a place of fascination, offers possibilities for restoration of direct attention (Kaplan and Kaplan, 1989; Hartig et al., 1991; Kaplan, 1995; Taylor et al., 2001, Kuo and Sullivan, 2004).

Direct contact with nature leads to improved self-concept, reduction of negative feelings, alleviation of symptoms of anxiety (Frumkin, 2001; Bingley and Milligan, 2004; Douglas, 2005). |
| Staying safe | Playing in attractive natural spaces enables children to develop a range of problem solving and risk assessment skills (Cornell et al., 2001). Ranging in local environments supports the development of cognitive mapping skills to enable children to find their way around (Hillman et al., 1990; Rissotto and Tonucci, 2002).

The provision of 'sensitively' adult managed play spaces offers children the opportunity to access natural elements while reassuring children and their carers (Best Play, 2000).

Children and young people use natural sites for developing 'special places' that exist as havens; attachment to these places supports self-regulation and renewal of cognitive capacities needed to process events and experiences that challenge and to balance pleasant and unpleasant emotions (Korpela and Hartig, 1996; Korpela et al., 2002). |

ECM outcome	Play, naturally – research evidence
Enjoying and achieving	Children's play is essentially about emotional enjoyment and peace that may also have 'trickle down' benefits (Sutton-Smith, 2002, 2003). The affordance of natural play spaces offers a rich and complex environment for the full range of play types and mechanisms (Hart, 1979; Moore, 1986, Hughes, 2001; Rasmussen, 2004) and associated benefits that arise from this diversity of play experiences. Contact with nature supports identifying, classifying, naming, sorting ideas and giving meaning to natural objects and spaces (Chapuniuk 1995; Wells, 2000; Tranter and Malone, 2004). The natural world provides an unlimited source of stimulation that is unique in the engagement of the senses and emotions (Cobb, 1977; Sebba, 1991). Such sensations may provide powerful memories that can be drawn upon in later life to maintain well-being (Chawla, 1990).
Making a positive contribution	Playing in natural spaces supports children's attachment to their local environments. Research indicates that playing in natural spaces is important for developing environmental awareness (Bixler et al., 2002; Wells and Evans, 2003; Wells and Lekies, 2006). Children's use of their local spaces builds an appreciation of natural systems and a sense of connectedness, supporting a sense of imagination and creativity (Cobb, 1977; Cohen, 1994). Children should be encouraged, through active participation in their local environments, to contribute to developing child-friendly environments (Hart, 1997; Chatterjee, 2005). Children are active agents and can articulate what they value in their local communities when appropriate methods are used to elicit their preferences (Rasmussen and Smidt, 2003; Burke, 2005; Karsten, 2005).
Economic well-being	The design of local communities that supports children's diverse play needs is beneficial to all inhabitants, creating safe and vibrant streets and communities (Franklin and Connolly, 2003). The possibility of a 'good childhood' (Moss and Petrie, 2002) and a child's sense of wonder may be linked to developing a sense of imagination and creativity (Cobb, 1977; Chawla, 1990).

Figure 3.3   Summary of evidence and links with ECM outcomes

Introduction

Factors that impact on children's access to natural and local spaces are complex. Again we must be wary of portraying universal patterns – as highlighted at the start of this review, each child, as an active agent, negotiates their way through the terrain and relationships of their own individual childhoods.

Yet a child's ability to do this will also be constructed and constrained by wider discussion about children and adults. Ward (1978) acknowledges that children are expert at creating their play niches within the urban landscape, in spite of the best efforts of adults to regulate and order this process; the ultimate truth is that 'children play anywhere and everywhere' (Ward, 1978:204). The popular adult opinion about the contemporary conditions for children's access to natural environments may not match how children actually carry out their play transactions in spaces. Elsley

(2004) talks of a potential mismatch between parents' and societies' views and beliefs about children's relationship and use of public space and the experiences of children themselves. Equally, Harden (2000) notes that children develop many strategies for subverting adult and legal prohibitions to negotiate their local environments.

As such, we should recognise that the nature of childhood (and adulthood) is constantly being negotiated and re-negotiated; that childhood is 'affected by and destabilised by contemporary social, technological and economic change' (Prout, 2005:33).

Bearing this in mind, we can identify some broad themes that are relevant to children's opportunity to play in natural environments. Orr (2002) outlines how the current pervasive political economy has transformed the lives of children from:

- Direct contact with nature to an increasingly abstract and symbolic appreciation of nature.
- Routine and daily contact with animals to contact with 'things' – inanimate, technological products.
- Immersion in community to isolated individualism.
- Less violence to more violence.
- Direct exposure to reality – and adventure and challenge – to an abstraction and virtual reality.
- A relatively slow pace to a relatively fast one.

Again we may see an emerging pattern over time through a number of studies expressing concern that children are spending less time outdoors (Nabhan and Trimble, 1994; Aitken, 1994; Hillman and Adams, 1992; Moore, 1997, Valentine and McKendrick, 1997, Waiton, 2001; Karsten, 2005; Louv, 2005).

The risk averse society

Lupton (1999) notes that at the end of the twentieth century the subtle distinctions between 'risk' and 'uncertainty' and 'good risk' and 'bad risk' have tended to be somewhat lost. With this blurring of terms has been an associated conflation of risk as meaning 'danger' and high risk means a lot of danger.

Adams' (2003) review of the nature of risks and risk assessment highlights the significance of 'virtual risk'. Virtual risks are socially or culturally constructed; when science cannot settle an argument, individuals are liberated to argue from pre-established beliefs, convictions and prejudices. They may or may not be real, but beliefs about them have real consequences. Modern society seems inherently more risky than in the past; we now live in a 'risk society' (Beck, 1992; Furedi, 2002). Virtual risks predominate parental concerns, and these are highly influential factors in children's opportunity to access independent play (Valentine and McKendrick, 1997).

Valentine's (2004) questionnaire and interview research with parents over a two-year period identifies that parents' fears largely relate to children of primary school age, with fear of abduction (45 per cent) and traffic accidents (34 per cent) being the highest concerns.

Hocking and Thomas (2003), in their analysis of childhood today, examine the significant impact that risk aversion has on children's lives, particularly where there is a growing 'privatisation' of childhood in which the responsibility of looking after children clearly lies with the family with an associated reduction in any form of community responsibility for children. Living in a 'culture of fear' puts parents in a difficult position as they make decisions about childcare practices such as how far from home their children may go when alone or with a friend or what particular places are declared off-limits. Many parents may well base these decisions on what amounts to over-estimation of risk and unfounded fear (Spilsbury, 2005). Valentine (2004:19) notes that whereas parents express great fears about their children's safety in public space, many acknowledge that the risk of being abducted is low or fairly low yet 'despite this recognition most still opt to restrict their children's play because the consequences of not doing so and losing a child make the risk not worthwhile'.

Key fears identified through research focus on:

- 'The bogeyman syndrome' (McNeish and Roberts, 1995; Moore, 1997; Waiton, 2001; Valentine, 2004; Louv, 2005; Spilsbury, 2005).
- Fears of traffic (Hillman et al., 1990; Huttenmoser, 1995; Moore, 1997; Mattson, 2002; Franklin and Connolly, 2003; Valentine, 2004).
- Moral panics (Valentine and McKendrick, 1997; Valentine, 2004).

Working in combination, parental fears for children's safety in outdoor spaces are 'constructed and mobilized through the media, vicarious experiences, "community" and educational campaigns' (Valentine, 2004:29). While there is a wealth of research exploring the consequences of this for children (see below), there is less evidence of the impact on the lives of parents/carers. Dixey's (1999) exploration of the impact of the 'culture of fear' highlights the normalised lengths that parents go to protect their children, expressing anxiety, stress, paranoia and being 'worried to death' about child safety. Such stress inevitably has an impact on the psychological well-being of parents.

Hughes (2001) expresses concern that current pressures on parents may act to prevent many children's access to traditional forms of play. For example, a report commissioned by Persil (2005) identified that nearly two-thirds (62 per cent) of parents were worried that they would be seen as a bad parent if their children were seen wearing dirty clothes. Consequently 72 per cent of children reported that they worried that they would be told off for getting dirty, and 14 per cent totally avoided any messy or outdoor activity. Thus children, through their parents' attitudes, may be becoming increasingly dirt, as well as risk, averse.

However, many parents still have positive childhood memories of playing outdoors with nature and recognise the value of such experiences for their own children (Clements, 2004). The combination of societal fear and personal aspiration creates a 'parent paradox', that may be key to changing wider attitudes around children's freedom to play.

Adult attitudes towards children outdoors

The 2003 Playday survey commissioned by the Children's Play Council investigated children's experience of adult intolerance when playing outdoors. The summary report revealed that:

- Four out of five (80 per cent) of children have been told off for playing outdoors.
- Half (50 per cent) have been shouted at for playing outdoors.
- A third (32 per cent) of seven- to 11-year-olds say being told off stops them playing outside.

The most common reasons for being told off cited by children were 'making a noise' and 'being a nuisance'. Similarly a MORI survey cited in Worpole (2003) found that 75 per cent of adults supported a legally enforceable curfew on teenagers outdoors.

Vanderbeck and Dunkley (2004), in their introduction to a series of articles on exclusion and inclusion of young people, acknowledge that children are excluded from full participation in activities and spaces both through the legal frameworks and everyday practices that reinforce the natural authority of adults. Even in rural areas children are discouraged from claiming spaces for themselves (Giddings and Yarwood, 2005). The introduction of legal processes to curb children's and young people's access to public space has arisen from a 'moral panic', as Valentine (1996) observes, that arises from a perception of children as being dangerous and out-of-control. Curfews reassert the 'adult spatial hegemony' (Collins and Kearns, 2001:401), keeping young people in their place and claiming basic human rights as adult-only. Louv (2005) refers to this process as the 'criminalisation' of natural play.

Several studies discuss the conflict between children's and adult value of space, noting the adult desire for safety, order and visibility contrasts with a child's desire for disorder, cover, loose materials, etc. (Jones, 2000; Rasmussen, 2004; Thompson and Philo, 2004). Pyle (2002) describes the 'vacant lot' as the potential open ground for children's explorations and contact with nature, a special place of childhood memory, and the differing adult perspectives on these spaces. To a child, this site is anything but 'vacant', but provides the opportunity for discovery, imagination and adventure. Yet to many adults, this is a dangerous and 'wasted space'. 'In a word the young and the grown often have different values about open ground' (Pyle, 2002:306). Ross's (2004) study highlights the significance of 'unkempt' areas for children's play, yet often these were the places that parents did not like their children to visit.

Reduction in ranging

A considerable amount of research over the past few decades indicates that children's opportunity to range independently has considerably diminished (Karsten and Van Vliet, 2006). Van Vliet (1983) reports that in a study of children over nine years in the UK, it was found that over 80 per cent owned bikes, but only 2.5 per cent were allowed to ride these to school. Van Vliet's (1983) study also comments on differences in opportunity to range between children in the suburbs and inner city, with children in suburban areas being able to move over wider areas. The report also notes differences between girls and boys ranging abilities. Moore's (1986) research with eight- to 12-year-olds supports Van Vliet's findings in reduction of ranging. Gaster's (1991) study of generational change to children's access to their neighbourhood highlights some significant trends:

- An increase in the age at which children were allowed out without supervision.
- A reduction in the number and quality of settings visited.
- An increase in the number and nature of parent-imposed restrictions.
- An increase in the number of professionally supervised activities undertaken.

Gaster (1991) concluded that the degree to which the neighbourhood environment supports children's opportunity to play out independently had declined substantially over three generations.

More recently, Tandy's (1999) study of the changing nature of children's outdoor play commented that mobility is a central issue if children are to have opportunities for investigative, exploratory and enjoyable play time. Tandy explores the changing pattern of children's bicycle ownership and use (as a key indicator of their independent mobility and freedom) and notes that while the ownership of bicycles has significantly increased, there is a drastic reduction in 'bicycle licence' – the adult granted permission to ride bikes in the local area. The study also shows that a high proportion of children surveyed named the home as their preferred play site, in response to parents expressed fears about the unsafe outdoors. Accompanying this is an inevitable decline in children's activity and associated health costs.

Rissotto and Tonucci's (2002) study of children's independent mobility in Italy drew attention to the prevailing trend in the Western world that as children's living conditions improved, there was a gradual reduction in their freedom of movement. Their research cites a 1997 study in which it was revealed that only 14 per cent of nine- to 11-year-olds interviewed said they always walk to school on their own, while 68 per cent said they were always accompanied by a parent. Their analysis of the different ways that children may move to school (independent walking, accompanied by an adult and driven) concludes that where children are allowed to walk independently to school, they had a much greater appreciation and knowledge of their local environment.

Other research largely supports this pattern (Wheway and Millward, 1997; Tuffin, 1996; Valentine, 1997; Valentine and McKendrick, 1997; O'Brien et al., 2000; Valentine, 2004).

Mackett and Paskins (2004) comment on the reduction in children's trips outside the home, with a decline of 4.7 per cent over a twenty year period to 2002, suggesting that children are leaving home less in their free time.

O'Brien et al.'s (2000) research with 10- to 11-year-old children in a variety of urban settings suggests that, compared with previous studies (Hillman et al., 1990) there has been a further reduction in children's independent use of public space. Similarly, Karsten (2005), using oral history, statistical and archive research, detects a new form of childhood that is evidenced through a decrease in playing outdoors and an increase in adult supervision. O'Brien et al. (2000) comment that there are significant variations in children's spatial lives – a reflection of a complex patterns of relationships and suggest marked inequalities in gendered and racialised patterns, a conclusion also reached by Karsten (2003) in her review of playground use in Amsterdam. Karsten (2005:287) concludes:

> ... that over time, public space has been transformed from a space that belongs to children (child space) into one meant for adults and accompanied children only ... The amount of time that urban children spend playing outdoors has declined considerably. While children used to be outside for hours at a

time and often participated in large groups, nowadays playing outside is much more limited in time, company and activity. Their use of public space to play and to socialize and their freedom of movement have decreased, although not for all children and not for all neighbourhoods to the same degree.

Karsten (2005) asserts that the changing nature of childhood not only deprives them of first-hand outdoor experiences but also separates them from children from diverse backgrounds.

This complexity of children's agency and spatial relationships is also evident in a number of recent studies that seek to move beyond universal patterns to exploring the intricacies of children's everyday lives. For example, Pooley et al. (2005) comment on the variability of children's independent mobility on the journey to school. While noting the increasing proportion of children (10- to 11-year-olds) travelling to school by car, there is still a significant proportion who will walk to school. The most interesting change can be found is the 'increasingly complex lives led by parents and other family members' (Pooley et al., 2005:52). Thus, for example, journeys to school may be connected with other activities and this impacts on both the nature of the journey and the mode of transport. What is also evident from Pooley et al.'s research is the tension between parents' concerns that children should move directly to and from school, while children prefer to use the walking time for playing and socialising.

Similarly, studies by Ross (2004), Armitage (2004) and Burke (2005) suggest that there may be a discrepancy between public opinion and perceptions about children's play and what children actually do in their local environments.

Armitage (2004) notes that the children questioned in the Hide and Seek (2001/02) study reported very few restrictions placed on them when it came to playing out. This is supported in Ross's study of children's play in Fife.

These contrasting studies perhaps indicate the complexity of this issue and the fact that children do actively negotiate their way through their local spaces. This challenges the notion of the 'unitary public child' (O'Brien et al., 2000) and proposes a perspective of heterogeneity in which children and young people construct a variety of meanings and understandings about their relationship to the environments in which they live (Nairn et al., 2003).

What should be of primary importance to adult designers of public space is an understanding of children's agency; the strategies they employ to access their preferred spaces and how this is accommodated in the prevailing adult agendas and interests (Burke, 2005). As such, it is important it is to find out young people's own views and experiences of their environments because 'these views are, first, diverse and not unitary and, second, challenge deterministic accounts of young people as automatically excluded from public space' (Nairn et al., 2003).

Colonisation of children's lives

Nowadays it is not unusual for children to be accompanied everywhere by an adult. Again, there is a historical context to this as Hillman et al.'s (1990) study highlights, noting the ever increasing escorting of children's school and leisure journeys that continues until an ever-later age.

Valentine and McKendrick's (1997) research notes that the perception that children are spending more time indoors may be misleading; what is changing is that children are spending more time under adult supervision. Hocking and Thomas (2003) comment on the increasing 'colonisation' of children's lives: the constant need to ensure that children are accompanied by adults. They highlight two significant consequences of this:

- First, it increases the organisation of children's time, with associated programme pressures and decreases in children's self-directed time, the times when children exercise their imagination, curiosity and creativity (Ennew, 1994; Christensen, 2002).
- Second, the increasing control of children's time and movements by parents leads to a 'censorship' of possible behaviours. Parents are more likely to foster, promote and organise those activities they deem to be appropriate for their children. Parental understanding of what is likely to be appropriate will reflect the societal and commercial pressures that prevail at any time, particularly through educationally desirable activities and a sanction of what is deemed to be risky and unsafe (Mayall, 2002).

Here we can see the ever-increasing 'field of constrained action' (Kytta, 2004 – see Appendix 2) impacting on a child's 'field of free action', giving rise to glasshouse and cell-like local environments.

Rasmussen and Smidt (2003) highlight the profound changes to childhood through the process of institutionalisation, an increasing trend in which more and more of children's activities take place in organised settings. In a later article, Rasmussen (2004) identifies three basic sites for children in their daily lives each represented as corners of the 'institutionalised triangle'. In one corner can be found the home with one side of the triangle being formed by the route to school. The school marks the second corner, with the next side of the triangle being formed by the route from school to the recreational facility, with the final side being the route back home. Rasmussen's description of a child's daily routines (2004) shows the movement around this triangle and notes the settings are adult designed as 'places for children' and thus are constructed in terms of what adults think children should be doing in such spaces.

Zeiher's (2003) study of children's mobility in Berlin highlights the increasing location of children's places (planned and designed specific places for children) as 'islands' scattered through the fabric of the city. Zeiher explores how each child develops an 'individual temporalised life space' – a unique pattern of activity undertaken by the children in different locations often accompanied and escorted by adults.

McKendrick et al.'s (2000) study of the growth of commercial play places in the UK provides a detailed analysis of this trend specifically in relation to children's play. They argue that many aspects of children's lives have become 'commodified'. McKendrick et al. question the ability of children to be active agents in their use of commercial play sites. Their research indicates that children play a marginal role in both making decisions about visiting commercial play spaces and contributing information about the preferred site prior to decision making, and as such these 'playscapes are primarily being used to address the needs of parents' (McKendrick et al., 2000:312).

McKendrick et al.'s research also makes some interesting points about the nature of the child consumer and commercial play spaces. The notion that, to a large extent, such provision is not targeted to the child market, but is geared towards adult consumption may match much of the current 'play' provision established for children. The implementation of the National Child Care strategy has created a rapid growth in after-school clubs (Smith and Barker, 2000). In their study of the institutionalised nature of such provision, Smith and Barker note that the use of space, children's behaviours, and the play opportunities available are all controlled by adults.

Change in play patterns

Accompanying the increasing institutionalisation of children's lives, research indicates there is an inevitable change in children's play patterns (Karsten, 2005). Clements' (2004) study indicates that children today spend less time playing outdoors than their mothers did as children. This is supported by Wridt's (2004) analysis of changing play patterns across generations in an area of New York, commenting on the decline of children's access to open, public play spaces and the increase in indoor and supervised activities. A recent survey reports that statistically children in the UK spend more time watching TV than playing outside (Barnado's and Transport 2000). Similarly the Persil Positively Dirty report found that 88 per cent of UK children watch TV every day compared with 33 per cent of children who play in the garden every day. Grayling et al. (2002) identify that more than half of the children under the age of 16 have their own television and young people spend more time watching TV than any other European country. Other research would generally support these findings of children's increasing sedentary lifestyle (Fjortoft, 2001; Garbarino, 1995; Ebbeling et al., 2002).

However, this is not necessarily a desirable state for children, as Fjortoft (2001) acknowledges, citing research by Hansen (1999) that, when asked, four out of ten children expressed a wish for more physical activity and complained about the lack of suitable arenas for play and free time activities such as building dens, climbing and sliding. The Play Space Survey (Children's Society/Children's Play Council, 2001) indicates that children largely prefer playing out in unsupervised areas (park, street, playgrounds, etc.) but 61 per cent of the children interviewed expressed some concern about accessing these sites (bullying, fear of traffic, parents' fears of strangers, etc.). The Child Accident Prevention Trust (CAPT) believes that lack of safe play space near to children's homes contributes to the large numbers of children not allowed to play outside at all (Sheriff, 2001).

The prevailing progress rhetoric of play (Sutton-Smith, 1997), which sees play as a tool for adults to use in directing children's socialisation and learning, has given rise to changing expectations of play behaviours. Institutions often inhibit and sanction children's rough and tumble, communication, mastery and deep play behaviours (Hughes, 2001; Holland, 2003). Children's leisure time is increasingly regarded as time that should be spent productively rather than wasted on 'purposeless' activity in public space (Mattson, 2002; Childress, 2004; Valentine, 2004). This links with changing perceptions of children's acceptance in public spaces (Valentine, 2004: Karsten, 2005).

A number of studies have highlighted the mismatch between an adult construct of children's play spaces and what children value and prefer to do in their own time (Moore, 1989; Matthews, 1992; Rasmussen, 2004; Worpole, 2003; Hart, 2004; Thompson and Philo, 2004; Armitage, 2004). Matthews (1992) proposes that much of the traditional approach to planning for play, through providing segregated play spaces, is failing to meet the play needs of children. In a later article, Matthews (1995) notes that most large-scale environments are designed to reflect adult values and usages and leave little room for other perspectives and uses, leaving children marginalised in these spaces. Playgrounds most often substitute a narrow range of physical activity for the spontaneous play in diverse environments that children more naturally seek out. Not only do playgrounds fail to satisfy the complexity of children's developmental needs, they also tend to separate children from the daily life of their communities and associated benefits (Hart, 2004).

Accompanying this mismatch between adult design and child use, some research highlights the increasing reluctance of children to play out in public space (Tuffin, 1996; Valentine and McKendrick, 1997; Harden, 2000; Thomas and Thompson, 2004). Valentine and McKendrick (1997) note that boys are now generally more willing than in the past to spend time at home, citing the increase in games technology and their large appeal to boys in particular as a significant factor in this trend.

Harden (2000), in her study of children's perception of their public and private spaces, finds that children construct the home site as a place of safety and security and express concerns about their vulnerability in public space. Harden's research identifies that children see the public space as one of risk and threat, with expressed fears of getting lost, the nature and visual perception of the physical environment, and the people who may inhabit the public realm. Harden (2000:50) identifies a third site for children's understanding of place and risk: the 'local space', a space between the public and the private. Children interviewed expressed local spaces as those that are close to home and where the people are known.

While this space was not perceived to be as safe as the home, it was not as risky as the public places. This area of close proximity to home was a more fluid space and, because of the indeterminate nature of its boundaries, was subject to continually changing perceptions; particular incidents and events could alter the nature and use of this space.

Thomas and Thompson (2004:8) note 'assessing danger was the first priority for children when thinking about different environments and their preferences within them'. The report identifies a range of children's concerns and fears about being outdoors, listed here in order of frequency and emphasis:

- Traffic – largely related to children's direct personal experience.
- Strangers/criminals – this was a significant fear among children and one that children could not always articulate. The street was viewed as a dangerous place to be, with few children naming it as a place where they played.
- Being lost – the fear of getting lost, and so becoming more vulnerable to strangers, proved to be a strong deterrent to children breaking parental restrictions to ranging. Thomas and

Thompson (2004:8), in line with Thompson and Philo's (2004) findings, note there is evidence that children do not always tell parents exactly where they go.

- Bullying – this was often mentioned, although children gave few examples of personal experiences of this happening.
- Trains – the research was conducted during the terrorist attack in Spain, which clearly had an influence on children's fears. Alongside this, trains were seen as dangerous because of the potential for being in an accident.
- Terrorism – this was an issue particularly in the London cohort of the study. The report notes how children's place fears were particularly sensitive to high-profile stories and the media portrayal of these.

Extinction of experience

In looking at children's relationship with nature, and associated benefits, many researchers have highlighted the importance of direct and unmediated contact (Hart, 1979, 1997; Moore 1986; Rivkin, 1995, 1998; Kellert, 2002; Wells and Lekies, 2006).

Kellert (2002) proposes a number of types of contact available to children:

- Direct – as the word implies, direct contact with natural settings and non-human species.
- Indirect – physical contact but in a managed context.
- Vicarious or symbolic experience – the absence of physical contact with the natural world, where the contact is through representation.

Kellert (2002) stresses the importance of all types of contact and outlines the ancient lineage of vicarious contact with nature through stories, paintings, myths and legends. However, he raises a considerable concern about the apparent shifting pattern of less direct contact with rich natural environments and the substitution of mass media images. Rivkin's (1998) analysis of Dewey's educational ideals highlights the importance of primary experience with the natural world and concludes that without this direct contact, children's comprehension of the environment will be trivial, partial and accompanied by a 'lamentable rootlessness' (Rivkin, 1998:201).

The reduction in outdoor play opportunities may be part of a wider ranging issue where children's first-hand experiences are being restricted. For instance, reductions in school trips, outdoor learning and field courses are other noted changes (NFER, 2004). Hart (1997) warns of the over-reliance on environmental education to substitute for children's direct access. One environmental centre contacted during the course of this review, Hamsterley Forest Outdoor Centre in County Durham, anecdotally reported that their usage by school, play and youth groups has steadily decreased recently to the point where its existence is in jeopardy. If this is typical, the widespread loss of such rural sites set up for children to experience nature directly will further impact on future opportunities for direct experiences.

Pyle (2002:312) outlines the concept of 'the extinction of experience', a notion that suggests that contact with a diversity of experiences with nature leads to an appreciation of a complex environment and the potential to develop attachment to and care for such spaces. However, when this diversity is reduced, or children denied access then there is likely to be a reduction in attachment, followed by disaffection and alienation. Pyle comments 'The extinction of experience is thus a cycle whereby impoverishment begets greater impoverishment' (Pyle, 2002:315). As such, the extinction of experience is likely to have a significant and harmful impact on health and development.

Pyle (2002) comments on the changing nature of children's opportunity to play in and with natural spaces; that our evolutionary legacy can be found in children's atavistic pleasure in survival games. However, as such skills are now seen to be non-essential for survival, we place little value on it and do little to foster these forms of experience, leading to what Pyle refers to as 'nature illiteracy'. Coupled with this is the lessening of intimacy with natural space.

Declining quality of outdoor play spaces

Worpole's (2003) study of children's play outdoors, citing research from the Children's Society and Children's Play Council 2002 survey, notes that the majority of the 500 children surveyed described their local parks and playgrounds as 'boring'. Children also commented that they were not allowed to play with water (45 per cent), not allowed to climb trees (36 per cent), not allowed to play on climbing equipment (27 per cent) and not allowed to ride bikes or play on skateboards (23 per cent) (Worpole, 2003:3).

Thomas and Thompson (2004) assert that poor local environmental quality will reduce a child's opportunity to play and develop a sense of connection and affection for their environments. Similarly, the final report of the Urban Green Spaces Task Force, *Green Spaces, Better Places* (DTLR, 2002), highlights the value of green space while commenting on the decline in the quality of much of this provision.

Many children are put off using local green spaces by:

- poor quality and badly maintained spaces
- inadequate provision of facilities
- unsafe and unwelcoming atmosphere
- inaccessible sites.

The report makes a central recommendation that all the people of a city should have access to high quality parks and green spaces, and this is particularly significant for those people who live in disadvantaged areas.

Canter (1977) notes the gap between an environmental designer's conceptual system and the conceptual systems of those that are not in that role, and thus there is a 'great possibility for a mismatch between creator and user' (Canter, 1977:4). Research into children's play lives increasingly highlights an emerging picture of such a mismatch between children's play needs and behaviours and the adult response to supporting children's play in their local environments (Matthews, 1992; Freeman, 1995; Stoecklin, 2000; Percy-Smith, 2002; Armitage, 2004; Rasmussen, 2004). The increasing exclusion of children from accessing and living in diverse spaces, largely through risk and fear, and the substitution of this through distinct, single function and isolated sites may give rise to an increasing sense of isolation, frustration and alienation with their local environments (Worpole, 2003).

This is matched with a general level of dissatisfaction with public open spaces (CABE, 2005) citing a 2004 survey in Greater London in which two-thirds of mothers interviewed said they would never allow their children to play in parks unsupervised.

Moore (1989) notes that playgrounds in the United States were in a crisis, citing criticism that playgrounds were adult attempts to control children's behaviour, as irrelevant to children's development needs and viewed by children as 'boring, hurtful and anti-social'. The physical environment in such spaces was often human made asphalt, with metal play structures, and little or no vegetation or access to natural elements. Johnson (2004) supports this picture with an assertion that 'adventure' is a missing component from the large majority of children's playgrounds – trees are not climbable, children are not allowed to create dens, build tunnels, play with mud or find secret hiding places. In seeking to meet their play needs, children are reduced to 'deviant' ways of finding adventure in these sites.

The human-made structures that predominate much of the children's playgrounds are generally viewed as 'boring' by children after initial use. The standardised arrangements offer no challenge or need to concentrate on movement (Noren-Bjorn, 1982; Nebelong, 2002; Blinkert, 2004).

Consequences for children's health and well-being

One particular consequence of an apparent reduction in children's opportunity to play outdoors may be identified through the current concerns about children's health, both mental and physical. Boseley (2005) reports that there are over one million obese children under 16 living in the UK – a third of the total in Europe. The British Medical Association (BMA, 2005) attribute this to the two key issues of changing eating patterns and levels of physical activity. The report notes that there is relatively little direct evidence (compared with adults) linking physical inactivity in children with childhood health outcomes but maintains that physical activity is important for bone health and development. Exercises that produce physical stresses on the bones during the years of the growth spurt can help to increase bone mineral density and protect against osteoporosis in later life. Children may engage in physical activity through play and recreation, which further enhances their social and mental health as well as their physical growth (BMA, 2005:20).

Kelso (2002), writing in the *Guardian*, highlights a report from the British Heart Foundation that indicates that a third of under-sevens fail to reach the recommended activity levels, and that by the age of 15, two-thirds of girls are classified inactive.

Key factors in this decline in children's physical activity are attributed to the increased use of cars for chauffeuring children, the reduction in likelihood that children can play outside (for reasons previously outlined) and the increase in more sedentary activities such as playing computer games (Fjortoft, 2001; Dietz, 2001; Ebberling et al., 2002; Mackett and Paskins, 2004).

However, this current concern is not entirely new. Armstrong's (1993) report of a study of 163 girls and 103 boys between the ages 11 and 16 found that 77 per cent of the boys failed to experience a single twenty-minute episode at the intensity equivalent to health-related physical activity, and that this rose to 88 per cent for the girls. Armstrong noted that children in the study had low levels of habitual physical activity and many children seldom experienced intense physical activity associated with health-related outcomes.

Veitch et al. (2005) in their study of children's play sites conclude that the opportunities for children's independent mobility and free play may be limited for many children. They find the results alarming 'as active free play is quite likely to be an important component of children's overall physical activity' (Veitch et al., 2005:9). This would certainly find support from Fjortoft's (2001) study of young children's play in a natural playground in Norway and the positive correlation between motor fitness in children. Similarly, Dietz notes 'opportunities for spontaneous play may be the only requirement that young children need to increase their physical activity' (Dietz, 2001:313). Ebbeling et al. (2002) suggest a significant contribution to prevention and treatment of childhood obesity can be made through protecting open space, and building parks and playgrounds. Mackett and Paskins (2004) note the difference between structured and unstructured use of children's time: structured time (going to clubs and tuition) generally requires travelling by car, whereas children's unstructured time will see children walking. They conclude their study with 'letting children go out to play is one of the best things that parents can do for their children's health'.

Sturrock et al. (2004) note that if evolution has equipped children with an incredibly rich and diverse play repertoire for making sense of themselves and their environments, any attempt to control or subvert this is likely to have a cost for the child. Yet, this is now a regular feature of adult intervention in children's lives, the 'play nicely' approach (Lester, 2005). Hughes's (2001) exploration of play deprivation suggests the impact of reducing children's opportunity for play may have potentially adverse effects on children's development. Hughes (2001:217) refers to the extreme of play deprivation as a 'chronic lack of sensory interaction with the world, a form of sensory deprivation'. This may be evidenced in the research carried out by Chugani et al. (2001) of post-institutionalised Romanian orphans which highlights the significant impairment to brain development caused by the stress of 'global deprivation'. Significantly, Chugani et al.'s study indicated that the results of continuous stress has severe impact on the children's limbic brain regions, and this may have altered the structure of this network giving rise to persistent behavioural disturbances.

Summary

Louv (2005) refers to the phenomenon of 'nature-deficit disorder' as a shorthand expression of the increasing distance between children and nature and associated consequences; 'diminished use of the senses, attention difficulties and higher rates of physical and emotional illnesses' (Louv, 2005:34). The impact of nature-deficit disorder may be viewed at individual, family and community level.

This review of the research into the contemporary conditions of childhood and its impact on children's opportunity to access natural spaces would suggest that children are finding it increasingly difficult to spend unmediated time playing in their local environments. The changing nature of children's lives may lead to a sense of dislocation and alienation from their immediate environments. Contributing factors to this are complex and interwoven, as outlined in the introduction to this section. There is also a tendency for this to be a self-reinforcing picture, creating myths and beliefs about the contemporary condition of children and childhood that perhaps masks the reality of their lives.

As some research has clearly indicated, children are very good at finding time and space to meet their own play needs (Wridt, 2004; Armitage, 2004; Burke, 2005). O'Brien et al. (2000) note that children 'make do' and get by in their lives in the city. The sophistication of children's competence to negotiate is often overlooked in the search for universal patterns (Ward, 1978; Valentine, 1997; O'Brien, 2000). Thompson and Philo (2004:119) illustrate this with an interview with a child who confesses:

> I'm not allowed down at the burn (stream), in case I get wet, but I still go.

Ward (1978) in his study of the child in the city almost thirty years ago acknowledged that some children are capable of exploiting everything their environment has to offer, can creatively manipulate their surroundings and thrive, but equally there are many who 'never get a foot on the ladder' and are isolated and alienated from their local environments. Blinkert (2004) maintains that unless we make efforts to improve the environmental situation for children, if children do not have the opportunity for creating experiences of their own, then 'one must fear for their development into creative human beings' (Blinkert, 2004:110).

Equally, Noren-Bjorn (1982) over two decades ago suggested:

> ... playing was a natural part of life. Opportunities abounded. Children had easy access to the places where adults worked, to animals and to nature. Unfortunately, however much of this has now changed. Children today often live in special environments, quite cut off from the working world of adults and from nature as well. They must be compensated for this loss by being offered a play environment rich in opportunities and experience.
> (Noren-Bjorn, 1982:11)

We may find through the evidence reviewed to date that the concerns expressed by Noren-Bjorn have become significantly more urgent. The notion of providing compensatory play spaces and opportunities is considered in the final section of this review.

Supporting children's opportunities to play in natural space

Introduction

Several studies note the benefits of children having outdoor experiences and the current constraints on children's access to spending time out-of-doors (Rivkin, 2000; Moore and Wong; 1997; Herrington and Studtmann, 1998; Karsten, 2005). Whilst many of the restrictive societal attitudes and public policies around children being outdoors need to be challenged (Gill, 2005), not all are likely be changed in the immediate future. Therefore compensatory spaces and opportunities are required to support and restore children's ability to play in and around natural spaces.

The notion of providing play spaces for children is not a new idea. Cranwell (2003) provides a valuable introduction to the history of play provision and notes that from as early as the 1830s reformers were advocating the importance of open space. The tradition of developing play provision provides an insight into the prevailing perspectives about children and the desired purpose of designing play spaces – largely as a way of providing welfare, education and control of children in working class areas. Gagen's (2000) review of the history of the US playground movement also highlights the drive for playgrounds as a form of acculturation into desirable social norms and roles. Hart (2004) comments that the history of planning children's play spaces in New York represented a felt need to contain children, to keep them off the streets, safe from traffic and unsavoury influences.

The need for space to play is recognised in the 'Six Acre Standard' (NPFA, 2001) that acknowledges:

> *Outdoor playing space for children is essential for their healthy development and accordingly, specific allocations have been made within the overall playing space standard for this purpose. Children are significant users of the outdoor environment and especially those areas adjacent to the family home. Consequently they comprise the group in greatest need of opportunities and well-designed environments for play.*
>
> (NPFA, 2001:24)

The NPFA clearly establishes some basic principles for the development of children's play spaces through:

- A local area for play (LAP) – a small area of open space designed and laid out for young children to play close to where they live.
- A local equipped area for play (LEAP) – an open space that is designed for children of early school age, located near to home (within 5 minutes walk).
- A neighbourhood equipped area for play (NEAP) – a space designated for use by older children, but can support younger children's play (located within 15 minutes walking time from home).

In his review of children's lives in the city, Ward (1978) expressed a concern that simply designating a site on a map as a play space does not guarantee that children will use this for its intended purpose. Ward advocated an approach that incorporates the claims of children to be admitted to all aspects of the city, and that the whole environment must be planned with children's needs in mind. Ward's plea might find a voice with contemporary commentators on children's relationship with planned play spaces (Freeman, 1995; Thompson and Philo, 2004; Worpole, 2003).

Alongside the design and provision of play spaces there has been a long tradition of developing supervised play provision in the UK. Here, awareness of children's instinctive drive to play and the role of stimulating environments for play are crucial in allowing child-centred experiences that allow playful encounters with nature. The diversity of providers and approaches for such environmental play provision is explored below.

Perhaps fuelled by the restrictions on children's access to outdoor play, the awareness, knowledge and enthusiasm for designing naturalistic play environments and facilitating children's natural play experiences appears to be growing (Maudsley, 2005; Gill, 2005).

Planning for natural play

Freeman (1995) comments that the prevailing approach to planning for children's play focuses on the provision of specifically designated play areas and argues that there is an urgent need to step back from this approach and to recognise the importance of the informal and natural environment as spaces for children's play.

Thompson and Philo's (2004) research indicates that what children get up to in their immediate environments is different from adult perception of how children should be spending their time. Given this, it is unlikely that adults alone will be able to design suitable outdoor spaces to meet the needs of children. Their research indicates that what children and young people want is spaces less for doing and more for being. Rasmussen (2004) comments that adult planners of children's space have forgotten what their own childhood play lives were like. Percy-Smith's (2002) detailed study of children and young people's use of local space concludes that catering for young people's local environment needs is not simply a matter of providing one or two 'token opportunities…but providing an environment in which young people are free to engage in a range of activities and place uses according to their own values, needs and creative potential' (Percy-Smith, 2002:63).

Chatterjee (2005) also comments on the need for children to have access to spaces that are diverse, many and spread out in the living environment of the child rather than having access to one site.

The Institute of Leisure and Amenity Management (ILAM, 2001) comments that the NPFA Six Acre standard fails to address the nature of children's local play needs through planning play spaces without taking into consideration the wider community issues of safe streets. The continued priority for traffic, and the decrease in cycling and walking does little to meet children's and parents needs. ILAM call for considering a 'trade-off' between safe play provision and safe streets for play to encourage a more creative approach to designing to support children's play needs.

Moore (1986) outlines a number of significant factors related to the preservation of children's domains and in a later article acknowledges that the key childhood environmental policy issues that emerged during the 1970s and 1980s have not changed much since that time (Moore and Cosco, 2000). Chief among these are the ideas of conservation of the special places of childhood, making streets liveable, urban wildlife management, the 'roughing up' of urban parks and greens and 'community animation'.

> ... *nature must be seen as an essential component of the experiential world of childhood, designed into every childhood habitat, providing daily immersion in nature, putting children in close touch with the biosphere. In the urban world we live in, implementation of this right cannot be left to chance. It is a design imperative.*
>
> (Moore and Cosco, 2000)

In looking at children's play needs, Worpole (2003) draws a distinction between formal public space and community space, noting that formal public space is expected to be well managed, clean and to appeal to everyone. The universal appeal of public space may in fact be a myth, particularly when children are largely lacking in agency and are not readily accepted in such places. This contrasts with 'community space' that may appear scruffy but have a high affordance value for children. If it is recognised that children's play is not ordered and site specific, it follows that children need access to both forms of space (Worpole, 2003).

Natural features of children's outdoor play spaces

Nature is often cited as a valuable component in children's play environments (Sebba, 1991; Hart, 1997; Moore and Wong, 1997; Fjortoft and Sageie, 2000; Johnson, 2004; White, 2004). Moore (1989:100) comments that children can create their own worlds in natural settings:

> *Natural materials that are alive, ever changing and renewing themselves have very high play value. They stimulate imagination and fine muscle coordination through play with vegetation parts, sticks and dirt. They engage children in problem solving when making clubhouses from natural materials. They support large muscle activities through games like hide-and-go-seek played among bushes and weeds and in climbing rocks and trees.*

Sutton-Smith (1990) cited in Nabhan and Trimble (1994:9) would like to see children have more 'smells, tastes, splinters and accidents'. Sutton-Smith highlights the paucity of children's available play spaces, devoid of vegetation with which to form 'nests', and states that children clearly need a space that develops a sense of territory, boundaries, surfaces and textures. Nabhan and Trimble (1994) maintain that we need to find ways to redress the loss of wildness by providing opportunities to gain access to vegetation and earth; to allow children to tunnel, climb and even fall. Fjortoft and Sageie (2000) criticise much of the current influential design factors for planning children's playgrounds that are often related to proximity and access rather than an appreciation of children's needs for a diverse and stimulating playscape.

Noren-Bjorn (1982), based on an in-depth study of playground use in Sweden identified a range of features that are likely to prove attractive to children in any play space and this is still entirely relevant to the planning of children's contemporary play space (see Appendix 5 for details).

Children, as Wheway and Millward (1997) note, spend much of their time passing through places, wandering and stopping off to play rather than as predetermined destinations. The alternative to this is isolation of children's sites and the need for children to constantly plan their time and social relationships (Zeiher, 2003).

Through their work on design of outdoor play settings, White and Stoeklin (1998) identify the elements children like in their play environments, including:

- Water.
- Vegetation, including trees, bushes, flowers and long grasses.
- Animals, creatures in ponds, and other living things.
- Sand, best if it can be mixed with water.
- Natural colour, diversity and change.
- Places and features to sit in, on, under, lean against, and provide shelter and shade.
- Different levels and nooks and crannies, places that offer privacy and views.
- Structures, equipment and materials that can be changed, actually or in their imaginations, including plentiful loose parts.

Outdoor play strategies

The Department for Culture, Media and Sport (DCMS) published the report *Getting Serious About Play* (2004), making a series of recommendations on the use a specific allocation of National Lottery funding for 'improving children's play opportunities' through a new, dedicated children's play programme. A key recommendation in the report is for local authorities to initiate a strategic inter-departmental approach to planning and supporting children's play.

(The Children's Play Council (2006) has produced a guide to support the process of developing local play strategies.)

McNeish (2005) notes that few of us would deny the importance of play, yet for today's children, the opportunity for play is becoming increasingly rare. Citing factors previously outlined, McNeish asserts that children's play is highly restricted and increasingly controlled by adults and concludes that opportunities for free play, enabling children to use public space as fully participating members of local communities, and promoting the development of open, accessible, green environments 'must be promoted as policy priorities nationally and locally':

> There is one area of policy for children – that of ... play and children's use of their local environments – where we both have sound evidence from research and clear and consistent messages from children themselves. Surely then, our policy response will reflect this evidence. So far, in Britain, this does not seem to be the case. Whilst we have a plethora of policy initiatives aimed at protecting children in the private sphere of family life, there is a dearth of attention paid to providing children with safe, child-friendly spaces in their local communities.
>
> (McNeish, 2005:115)

Moss and Petrie (2002) highlight the need to shift from a narrow development of purposeful places for children, usually single purpose, to a much wider appreciation of children as members of a local community and a recognition of their needs for a wide range of spaces; in developing this there is 'scope for many innovations, in particular making far more use of outdoor environments to support outdoor play and play provisions' (Moss and Petrie, 2002:179). In developing a local authority response to children's play it is important to place the diversity, complexity and richness of children's play lives at the heart of the strategy and to 'think beyond play equipment and kick-around pitches' (Children's Play Council, 2006).

Given the evidence presented through this research, a play strategy should start with recognition of what is known about children's play and what are the current barriers that impact on children's ability to play naturally within their local environments. As such, it will address those spaces that children use daily – playgrounds, parks, streets, schools, forecourts – the familiar territories of children's outdoor play lives (Worpole, 2003; Gill, 2005):

> My action plan for outdoor play would start with the spaces and places children find themselves in every day: playgrounds, parks, schools and streets. If what best feeds children's bodies, minds and spirits is frequent, free-spirited, playful engagement with

nature, we need to go with the grain of their play instincts and put our efforts into creating neighbourhood spaces where they can get down and dirty in natural outdoor settings, free of charge and on a daily basis.

(Gill, 2005)

Parks and natural playgrounds

Moore's (1989) critique of playgrounds highlights the general failure of many of the planned children's spaces to meet children's diverse play needs. Moore (1989) cites the work of Petersen (1985) who comments that the traditional playground does not provide for playing with elements, for caring contact with plants and animals, or for transforming and creating the materials and space to children's own needs.

Frost (2006), discussing playgrounds in the USA, comments that nearly all playgrounds for school-age children fall short on integrating garden and nature areas, constructive play materials and symbolic play props into outdoor play and learning environments. But there are a growing number of playground planners who are transforming the traditional playground into more 'naturalised' spaces. Frost (2006) cites the projects developed by Moore and Wong (1997) as a powerful example of the benefits of integrating nature into play spaces. Worpole (2003) gives some examples from the UK where local playgrounds and community spaces have been transformed by working with local children and adults. Frost (2006) contrasts the high cost and maintenance associated with 'mammoth, multi-tiered structures that have little play value' and the reduced expenditure associated with play spaces that use natural materials, plentiful loose parts and 'wisely selected built or purchased equipment' (Frost, 2006:14).

Moore (1989) contrasts this traditional approach with the adventure playground movement. The development of adventure playgrounds is generally attributed to Christian Th. Sørensen, a Danish garden and landscape architect and the development of 'junk playgrounds' in Emdrup, Copenhagen. From the beginning, these playscapes (Frost, 1992) had a lot more to offer than conventional playgrounds including construction play with various materials and other handcraft activities as well as animal husbandry and gardening (Ginsberg, 2000).

Playlink (2001) provides a rich collection of play stories from a variety of adventure playgrounds in London that clearly illustrate qualities associated with the place preference factors identified by Kaplan and Kaplan (1989) of mystery, challenge, coherence and legibility, for example:

Two boys, one carrying a packet of biscuits the other a bottle of coke, ran from their flats and across the grassy bank to the adventure playground. Once inside they made their way past children busy with hammers and nails, saws and paint, to a den made of wooden planks. A face popped out from the planking 'What's the password?' 'Abracadabra!' came the reply, and the two boys joined their friend in their den for their secret feast. Theirs was not the only den on the playground. Lots of them, all shapes, sizes and colours, were springing up on Kennington Playground as part of a project to involve the children in developing the outside play area. All of them contained groups of friends playing freely in their own private space.

(Playlink, 2001:17)

Similarly, Lester (2005) provides a range of reflective anecdotes from an adventure playground in Manchester, including the following:

After heavy rain, the sand under the big swings used to turn into huge puddles – which considerably added to the excitement of using the swing. On one occasion we watched a group of children, who had arrived directly from school and were fearful of getting their school uniforms dirty, attempt to drain the water away from the swing area using a spade and other found tools – sticks, a sheet of plastic. The children became more and more engrossed in the results of their actions – digging channels and seeing the effects, building dams to create waterfalls, moving into connecting with other puddles – and as more children arrived, they too joined in and soon the whole area became a network of canals, reservoirs, dams – the original intent lost through the play.

(Lester, 2005:237)

Chilton (2003) offers a valuable overview of the development of adventure playgrounds in the UK and current issues facing adventure playgrounds at the start of the twenty-first century.

Worpole's (2003) study agrees with the sentiments expressed by Petersen (1985). Worpole's review draws on the work of landscape architect Helle Nebelong (2002) and experiences in transforming play spaces in Denmark that has seen a greater emphasis on nature and less prefabrication. Amongst a multitude of benefits from this type of playground, Helle Nebelong highlights the importance of nature's 'knobbly and asymmetrical forms' for providing invaluable opportunities to develop skills associated with negotiating complex physical spaces (Gill, 2006).

In Stirling, following the inspiration from Helle Nebelong, local communities have teamed with the Council to produce more naturalistic and child-friendly play spaces (Gill, 2005).

Blinkert (2004) challenges much of the current design principles for constructing children's spaces. Applying the concept of 'action space', Blinkert suggests that much of the spatial provision for children is highly ordered and standardised. In countering this, Blinkert has worked with local communities in Freiburg in Germany to replace order with chaos through sites that are functionally unspecific, a place that does not offer predetermined possibilities, but provides an environment of high potential, where children can invent, create and improvise. The resulting play spaces look rather like an 'empty site which is somewhat neglected and unkempt' (Blinkert, 2004:106).

There are multiple benefits: child-centred, diverse and flexible play opportunities, cheaper capital costs, more sustainable materials and attractive to wildlife. The success is visible with many children using the newly created natural play spaces and they are attracting international attention (Gill, 2005).

The Forestry Commission are developing and expanding natural playgrounds within their woodland sites to encourage active play and further children's exploration of adjacent natural settings (Houston et al., 2006). Following feedback from visitors and advice from environmental play design specialists, the Eden Project, an innovative visitor centre in Cornwall celebrating people and plants, have also recently extended a natural play area with living willow and sand.

As with the above examples, Fjortoft and Sageie's (2000) study of how children played within a natural playground highlights the qualities within such spaces that support imagination, exploration and diversity of play types. The introduction to the article quotes a kindergarten child who comments: 'Climbing rocks is more fun than climbing trees – but climbing trees is more fun than the boring playground equipment' (Fjortoft and Sageie, 2000:83). They suggest that new criteria are developed that recognise affordances and challenges for children and note:

> In such a perspective it is necessary to discuss an acceptable level of risks. Playscapes with the highest level of security tend also to represent areas with the lowest affordances and challenges. Consequently, diversity in landscape elements, affordances for play, challenges and safety, accessibility and wear resistance may be important criteria in the planning and management of future playscapes for children ... The overall conclusion from the present study may be that natural landscapes represent potential grounds for playing and learning and this has to be taken into serious consideration for future policy and planning of outdoor grounds for children.
>
> (Fjortoft and Sageie, 2000:94)

The Commission for Architecture and the Built Environment (CABE) have promoted a number of campaigns and initiatives to improve public open green spaces and parks, including a drive to increase staffing in parks and urban green spaces. The 2004 report on involving children and young people in the design and building process contains a range of examples of attractive playgrounds and parks. The guide *Start with the Park* (CABE, 2005) acknowledges that there is an existing supply of public green space – parks, gardens, tree-lined streets, play areas, sports fields, green corridors, etc. – and this should provide the basis for a 'multifunctional green mosaic with an amazing variety of characters, functions, scales and settings' (CABE, 2005:14). The report accepts that, for many places, the need is not to create more green space but to optimise what already exists through ensuring sites are diverse and distinctive, provide function and conviviality and are accessible and connected.

The growing number of play ranger projects, which provide peripatetic playworkers in designated parks and public green spaces, offer valuable models of good practice. Here the emphasis is on:

- Working where children are already present.
- Providing a highly visible and regular staffed provision to help overcome parental fears of children being outside.
- Enhancing the space through planned activities and equipment.
- Building relationships with the children and facilitating child-centred play.

Environmental improvement of the spaces (as is now beginning to happen in consultation with the children for the Community Play Rangers at BANES) is preceded by establishing a regular pattern of usage for children's play.

School grounds

One of the few remaining opportunities for children to 'play out' at regular intervals is through school playtime (Blatchford, 1998; Factor, 2004; Tranter and Malone, 2004). Blatchford (1998) notes that school playtime is one of the few occasions when children can interact in a relatively safe environment, with little adult control and where the play and social relationships are largely in their control. Yet this time of playing naturally is being greatly sanctioned (Blatchford, 1998; Thompson, 2005). Increasingly the school play-time is seen by adults as a negative experience. Alongside this, there has been a reduction in the amount of time given over to 'play time' (Rivkin, 1995; Blatchford, 1998).

There has often been conflicting interest in the use of school grounds. Worpole (2003) comments that many schools have become institutional enclaves disconnected from the local community. Thomas and Thompson (2004) note that although 63 per cent of the educational sites are out of doors, it is estimated that school grounds are used to only 30 per cent of their potential. The introduction of the government's extended schools initiative, offering parents extended childcare, offers the potential to re-address some of these issues – but only if the key focus is on opening up the outdoor spaces for children's play (Children's Play Council, 2006). This means resolving the apparent tension between the adult perspective of neat and aesthetically pleasing sites and the preferred sites for children that includes loose parts to manipulate, long grass to play in and freedom to construct, change and cultivate the space.

Alongside these concerns, others have expressed the potential of the school playground as a significant response to children's dwindling opportunity to have meaningful contact with natural space (Moore, 1989; Titman, 1994; Moore and Wong, 1997; Herrington and Studtmann, 1998; Wilson, 2001). Wilson (2001) claims that for most young children the first public space that they encounter and develop intimate knowledge about is the school playground, citing Sebba and Churchman (1986) who note that the school yard offers freedom of movement, play, contact with natural elements and informal social contacts.

Rivkin sees the development of school grounds as a way of restoring children's opportunity for outdoor experiences and concludes that school playgrounds should be 'habitats', that is, places where children can live. Herrington and Studtmann's (1998) creation of an 'experimental' early years outdoor play space highlights how sensitive design and introduction of natural features can enhance children's developmental experiences and help establish a sense of place within the playground.

Wilson (2001) outlines key considerations for developing positive school playgrounds, identifying a number of key factors:

- Create and/or preserve natural areas around the school.
- Create opportunity for seclusion and quiet.
- Provide opportunities for active exploration.
- Encourage activities in which children can effect change.
- Build in diversity and complexity.
- Provide opportunities for immersion and immediate encounter with the natural environment.

Tranter and Malone (2004) provide a comparative analysis of two Australian schools and their playground use. One school (Orana) was committed to providing an attractive natural physical landscape for children with many distinctive natural features. While the second school (Aranda) had an equally attractive physical environment, it was limited in use by children due to boundary controls and off-limits areas. The study highlights the diversity of children's play behaviour in Orana, particularly through direct access to a range of natural spaces in which children amongst other activities, built dens and developed make-believe games using the range of natural features and loose materials. Burke (2005) makes similar observations about two school playgrounds in east Leeds, one of which was a far richer space due to the design elements of natural areas, trees, bushes and 'rough' areas. However, it was not possible for children to play in this site after school.

Tranter and Malone (2004) conclude that in the absence of children's access to natural space in the city, and the strong possibility that this is likely to remain the case in the near future, 'it is appropriate that attention is focused on enhancing children's use of their school grounds as a significant site for natural learning' (Tranter and Malone, 2004:153).

The importance and potential of school grounds as places for natural play and learning is championed in the UK by *Learning through Landscapes* (LtL), a national school grounds charity. LtL provides general advice and support on developing school grounds and runs a number of specific programmes to fund and facilitate environmental improvements in early years, primary and secondary schools. Further information can be found on their website: www.ltl.org.uk.

The awareness and practice of redeveloping naturalistic school grounds may be gaining momentum. A recent article in *Children Now* (NEWS Playgrounds: Play school, 3 May 2006) highlights the positive effects experienced by one of the schools funded by LtL to develop a natural play area, and suggests that many UK schools are following course.

The street

Moore (1987) highlights a number of primary reasons as to why street space is attractive to children, citing two key features:

1. The close proximity and ease of access represented by streets.
2. They offer linear play surfaces, often preferred by children for everyday games, particularly where time is at a premium.

The street generally does not get muddy; the smooth surfaces enable many opportunities for moving in different ways such as roller-blading, skateboards or cycling. Moore (1987) describes the street as an important arena for children's informal peer friendships and since walking is children's primary way of moving around the neighbourhood, they will use streets to get from one place to another. ('Walking' in this context involves all the different ways that children move through the streets – running, hopping, jumping, climbing and balancing on walls, etc.)

Moore (1987:53) describes the significant potential of the street site:

> The street is a world as exotic as it is familiar. There children play in the interstices between parked car, alongside the curbside ecotone of gutter rivers, down bottomless storm drains, among insect life of sidewalk verges, in jungles of front fence vegetation, and on grandstand stoops. Among the myriad and inexhaustible supply of toys are maple and sycamore seed helicopters, mayflower pea shooters, horse chestnut conkers, and wonderful rubbish put out for pick up… The street playground offers leaves for shuffling, railings and boarded fences to run sticks along, patches of dirt for constructing imaginary landscapes and occasional building materials, such as sand piles.

Huttenmoser (1995:2) noted that for living surroundings to become significant in children's daily lives they must be accessible, open for play and frequented by other local residents, especially children. Huttenmoser notes:

> Over the last few decades, living surroundings have gone through the most substantial reduction historically seen through heavy increase in street traffic (Huttenmoser, 1991). When living surroundings are not free from motorised traffic or when the vehicles do not drive slowly or take children into consideration, parents will not allow their children to play outside alone. For children, as well as parents, however, it is decisive that unaccompanied play be possible.

Generally, there is now a prevailing perception of these 'living spaces' as being unsafe and unsuitable for children and young people and this denies children access to a rich space that cannot be easily compensated for by alternative provision (Franklin and Connolly, 2003).

Research frequently notes the importance of immediate local space for children as places of transition from home to the outside world and from child to adolescent (Matthews, 1992; Matthews et al., 2000b; Thompson and Philo, 2004). As CABE (2004) highlight, public space provides sites for children to meet and play, to 'establish a world for themselves', to explore their immediate environments and negotiate their way from one site to another. Yet this may be little recognised or valued, a factor that children will often contest and stake their claims to using public spaces.

A recent analysis of the guiding principles for developing clean, attractive and safe streets can be found in the CABE publication, *Paving the Way*.

Another significant contribution to the redesign of street space can be found through the Home Zone movement. Originally pioneered in the 1970s in the Netherlands, but now in increasing evidence in many parts of the UK, home zones are an attempt to strike a balance between traffic and everyone else who uses the street, including local children. Details of this movement can be found at: www.homezones.org

Gill (2006) provides a useful summary of the recent Transport Research Laboratory evaluation of a limited number of Home Zone projects in England and Wales, noting considerable support for the schemes from adults and children, with five out of the seven evaluations suggest a 'positive impact on play opportunities and independent mobility of children and young people' (Gill, 2006:98).

Access to the countryside

In England, recent changes through the Countryside and Rights of Way Act, commonly known as the 'right to roam', have opened up large areas of the countryside to public access. The Land Reform Act has had similar implications in Scotland.

Although primarily promoted for walking and adventure activities, the access to countryside beyond footpaths has positive implication for outdoor recreation and some manifestations of children's play. More information is available from: www.countrysideaccess.gov.uk

Woodland sites

Through its Active Woods programme, the Forestry Commission encourages the use of public access woodland for diverse leisure activities, including children's play. As a highlight the FC has recently produced guidelines for site managers that proposes an open-minded and balanced approach to den building and rope swings, which only intervenes when children's safety is significantly compromised (Harrop, 2006). The FC website (www.forestry.gov.uk/active) allows local woodland sites and events to be searched for in England, Scotland and Wales. The positive attitude to play is highlighted through the FC's promotion of children's den building, e.g. through a national den building day.

The Woodland Trust (www.woodland-trust.org.uk) also has a directory of its woodland sites for public access, and a recent report *Space for People* outlines the Trust's commitment to providing woodland areas near to where people live.

Local nature reserves

WildSpace! is a grant scheme administered by English Nature (www.english-nature.org.uk) to promote and support local nature reserves and designate new ones with community involvement as part of the criteria alongside wildlife value. A general aim of *WildSpace!* is to promote the use and enjoyment of Local Nature Reserves and bring people and natural environments closer together. Local projects throughout England have stimulated a wide range of community participation, and through a combination of play, informal educational and family events allowed children to explore and experience local nature reserves close to where they live (see case study in Maudsley, 2005).

Country parks

Country Parks, generally owned or managed by local authorities, provide extensive and varied green spaces for public access and children's informal play. A dedicated website (www.countryparks.org. uk) allows the nearest country parks or specific sites to be searched for.

In some cases the role of such sites for play is actively supported, for example at Mersey Valley Countryside Warden Service (www. merseyvalley.org.uk). Manchester and Trafford Council manage 30 natural sites, which have public access. To encourage and promote children's play at these sites the warden service runs free environmental play sessions for playschemes during school holidays.

Play provision

A significant attempt to redress the loss of children's opportunity for unmediated play in their local environments has been made by the spread of adult organised play spaces – play centres, after-school clubs, adventure playgrounds, holiday playschemes, etc.

The growth of after-school provision, with the introduction of the National Childcare Strategy, has given rise to an increase in out-of-school clubs. Mayall and Hood (2001) suggest that the current government's out-of-school policy has raised key questions about the siting and staffing of such provision. They pose fundamental questions about the underlying (and often contradictory) principles underpinning these developments. Alongside this shift, there is also confusion about the assumed developmental benefits of children learning through play. This may be at odds with what children actually value in terms of their out-of-school lives (Lester, 2005).

Olds (2001:15) talks of organised play spaces (more specifically early years centres) as 'spirited places' and sites for making whole, to create places of freedom and delight, where 'the enchantment and mysteries of childhood can be given full expression' and 'satisfies children's souls'.

The way in which organised play provision has responded to children's needs and developed specific opportunities for them to engage with the natural environment through play, is explored through the concept of environmental play below.

Environmental play

Given that children spend considerable amounts of time in organised play settings, there is growing realisation of the role of high quality environmental play provision for meeting children's need for play with natural elements.

It may be argued that all children's play is environmental. However, environmental play has come to represent the relationship between children and natural environments through play, particularly in the context of adult-mediated provision.

Therefore 'environmental play' may be defined as:

> *Opportunities for children and young people to play freely with,*
> *in and around natural environments and elements.*
> (Maudsley, 2005)

The term seems to have evolved from environmental education and certainly appears to have arisen from working partnerships between play providers and environmental education organisations, including Wildlife Trust WATCH groups, in the 1980s (Earthkids, 1989). The underling aims of environmental play projects reflect differences in these two broad types of host organisation:

● Increasing play opportunities through access to natural environments

  and/or

● Raising environmental awareness in children through play.

In practice, however, these aims are not mutually exclusive, as Part 3 of this review elucidates. The net benefit has been a proliferation of approaches in providing children's free play in natural environments within the context of supervised settings.

The range of environmental play projects in the 1980s was illustrated in a 'guide to good practice' assembled by the Earthkids project based at the Urban Wildlife Trust in Birmingham (Earthkids, 1989). The project did not continue past its initial networking phase (Birmingham Wildlife Trust personal communication). Most of the host organisations reported in the guide are still in existence; however several of the specific environmental play projects do not seem to have survived, at least not in their original guise.

A highly significant aspect of environmental play both then and now has been the working relationships developed over a range of different sectors. These include:

- playwork
- environmental education
- nature conservation bodies
- outdoor leisure
- community groups.

Each sector brings different strengths to environmental play provision to provide a more robust whole. For instance, many environmental organisations have successful working practices for facilitating adventurous outdoor activities, whereas playworkers often have a well-developed child-centred approach.

Better Play, a funding programme from the New Opportunities Fund – now the Big Lottery Fund – and managed by Barnardo's, recently funded 14 specific environmental play projects. The range of projects was wide in terms of geographical spread, type of organisation and methods of working practice, and collectively generated a high degree of participation in environmental play. Output from the projects was summarised in a Better Play report on environmental play (Maan, 2005). Key messages from the report were:

- That children's health and well-being were positively influenced by environmental play opportunities.
- That children develop positive relationships with nature through play.
- The need for appropriate risk taking through environmental play.
- The importance of inclusive access to outdoor play environments.

Common issues included: transport to sites, litigation concerns and sustainability of project tenure. The latter issue is obviously related to long-term funding of such projects. Consequences to the end of Better Play funding has been varied including: non-continuation (e.g.

Northumberland Wildlife Trust), new lottery funding (e.g. Middlesbrough Environment City) and new ways of working (e.g. Herefordshire Nature Trust – service level agreements with housing associations).

Environmental play case studies

Whist it has not been possible to provide an extensive directory of environmental play provision within the scope of this review, a selection of illustrative projects are detailed below. Further information on good practice in environmental playwork is provided by Maudsley (2005), and other case studies of projects supporting adventurous outdoor activities for children and young people can be found in OPENspace (2006b).

The development of environmental play provision within county Wildlife Trusts has been an important and influential factor. A number of specific environmental play projects are currently hosted by Wildlife Trusts in:

- Herefordshire – www.wildlifetrust.org.uk/hereford
- Staffordshire – www.staffs-wildlife.org.uk
- Tees Valley – www.wildlifetrust.org.uk/teesvalley

The WildPlay project in Herefordshire has been a particularly influential environmental play project: running regular children's playschemes at the Wildlife Trust's natural sites, working as a detached play service on housing sites and running a training programme for other playworkers in the county. Their ethos and activities are documented on a DVD/CD-ROM available from the Wildlife Trust.

Many other Wildlife Trusts are incorporating the principles and practice of environmental play into their organisational roles. For instance, Avon Wildlife Trust has provided settings for environmental playwork training events and consequently included play in its education policy (Maudsley, 2005).

Similarly, many city farms and community gardens across the UK provide valuable settings for environmental play. These generally comprise small but ecologically diverse sites mainly within urban areas, which are accessible for children during specific organised sessions and/or for unsupervised play.

Bath City Farm

Includes a play ranger project based at the Farm (part of the BANES Community Play Rangers).

Blacon City Farm, Chester

www.chester.gov.uk/main.asp?page=417

As well as an adventure playground, the farm has a dedicated environmental play area where children can build dens, follow treasure hunts and explore wildlife.

St. Werbugh's City Farm, Bristol

www.stwerburghs.org

The farm has developed an abandoned orchard and pig farm in the city centre into a community green space with a regular environmental project for teenagers.

Significantly both the Wildlife Trusts (www.wildlifetrusts.org) and City Farms (www.farmgarden.org.uk) are supported by umbrella organisations that provide networking, information, advice and representation at national, regional and local levels. As well as a small number full-time staff, the National Federation of City Farms also maintains around 20 flexible fieldworkers to support individual projects as needed.

Adventure playgrounds have a long pedigree of providing engaging, child-centred outdoor play (Chilton, 2003), especially in connection with elemental play – playing with the natural elements of earth, air, fire and water. Some adventure playgrounds have developed natural spaces and elements to widen children's experience of nature through play provision, e.g. the nature playground at *Oasis Children's Venture* in London.

Skelton Grange, Leeds

www.skeltongrange.org.uk

Managed by BTCV Skelton Grange environmental education centre provides environmental playschemes during school holidays throughout the year and through Better Play funding has developed accessible play opportunities for disabled children. The centre also runs a Wild in the Woods programme to help build children's relationships with natural environments.

Greenstart (Groundwork Trust), County Durham

www.durhamweb.org.uk/chesterlestreetss/Greenstart.htm

An early years project working with Groundwork West Durham to pilot the creation and development of green play spaces in both rural and urban settings. The project also aims to link young children and their parents to natural environments through activity sessions in disadvantaged areas.

Green Explorers Play Together, County Durham

northernpeople@btopenworld.com

Initiated by a local community organisation to run outdoor play activities for disabled children, the project received Better Play funding to run an inclusive environmental out-of-school play provision. Now with HLF funding, the project is able to continue its work, including developing a nature garden.

Woodland Play Centre, Somerset

www.woodlandplaycentre.com

In 1999, Louise Kennedy set-up an environmental playscheme at a woodland site in rural west Somerset, to provide a range of inspiring naturalistic play opportunities as part childcare for local children. The running and outcomes from the project is documented in a video called *Playwork Take One* available from Playwork Partnerships: www.playwork.co.uk.

Swainswick Explorers, BANES

www.playingoutdoors.org

Similarly, this social enterprise childcare provision near Bath has developed high quality environmental play opportunities throughout the year, including tree-climbing, den-building, splashing in streams and campfire cookery (Maudsley, 2005).

Crucially, both Swainswick and Woodland Play Centre have gained ongoing access to a variety of local natural environments for children's play through building relationships with amenable landowners.

Wild About Play network

www.playwork.co.uk/wildaboutplay

Initially funded through Better Play and hosted by Playwork Partnerships, Wild About Play is a networking project to support and promote environmental play. The project ran a series of taster promotion/training sessions in environmental play across South West England, and has subsequently produced a number of resources including a practical guide to environmental playwork (Maudsley, 2005). The network database holds nearly 500 individuals and organisations interested in environmental play. In partnership with Herefordshire Nature Trust, Wild About Play organised the first UK-wide conference in environmental play; a second event is planned for July 2006.

The *Wild Things* Ecological Education Collective (www.wildthings.org.uk) also hosts a wild play network of groups in Nottinghamshire with a shared interest in encouraging children's learning and development through environmental play.

Maintaining free play within environmental play provision

It is easy for adults to become guardians, organisers and supervisors of play when outdoors with children. However, in order to meet children's wishes and meet their biological and developmental needs the value of freely chosen, child-centred nature play needs to be recognised and prioritised.

The ability of environmental play provision to facilitate children's free play in and with nature requires a number of interrelated components:

- That *all* adults involved in developing provision with children have a clear understanding of the nature of children's play, as summarised though the Playwork Principles (Play Wales, 2005). This incorporates awareness of the importance of children's instinctive play and recognition that opportunities for unadulterated play experiences can be provided even if they are not strictly adult-free.
- That children may have developed inappropriately negative or fearful attitudes to nature through lack of early experiences or as learnt behaviour from adults. In such instances guided or supported encounters with natural elements from playworkers may be needed as springboards for subsequent free play.
- There should be a feeling that the play setting is an open space (after Sibley, 1995) that has a recognised culture of play and can accommodate children at the margins, that values diversity of play behaviours and where the adults are clearly seen as supporters of this process.
- The provision should provide children with a 'field of free action' (Kytta, 2004), where children can independently discover and actualise the affordances that the setting offers to the child.

Environmental playwork training

The range of training opportunities for environmental playwork in the UK are detailed in Maudsley (2005). Currently there is no UK-wide

89

training programme in environmental playwork, although a number of different regions have developed local courses. Some of the principles and practices of environmental play are being incorporated into mainstream playwork education at various levels, e. g. the new Play Wales training programme.

The Play Officers Wales Network, supported by Play Wales, has run informal experiential training in elemental play called 'Mud and Sparks'. These were facilitated skill-sharing sessions in natural settings that allowed playworkers hands-on playful opportunities with natural elements such as mud, water, air and fires. The approach was both practical and empowering, allowing participants to explore their own interests and reactions in a supportive setting. Play providers were then able to go back and translate their own experiences into effective working practice with children. This approach illustrates the value of personal, direct experience in preparing for environmental play as highlighted by Maudsley (2006).

Playwork Partnerships in collaboration with Play Wales are currently writing a Level 2 course 'Playing with the Elements' that builds on these principles of learning by experience and aims to widen and support the provision of outdoor play across the playwork sector.

Forest Schools

www.foresteducation.org

A growing number of playworkers aspiring to develop environmental play provision are undertaking Forest School training. Having begun at Bridgwater College, this is now available across the UK through a range of accredited training providers (see Maudsley, 2005). The Forest School training 'curriculum' covers practical outdoor skills such as shelter-building, fire-lighting and use of tools and an ethos that aims to build children's confidence and self-esteem. There are large overlaps in approach with playwork in terms of being child-centred and experiential. There are also key differences in that Forest Schools follows a devised sequential programme over a series of sessions, whereas playwork follows a more flexible approach.

Summary and recommendations

The diverse research findings presented throughout this review have stressed the importance of children having access to natural, outdoor spaces for play. Thus, it becomes imperative that we acknowledge the nature of children's play and work towards developing appropriate settings and conditions for this to take place.

Chatterjee (2005) proposes a definition of child-friendly outdoor environments as places that promote:

… exploration and actualisation of its many affordances for different activities and social interactions; offers opportunities for environmental learning and competence by shaping physical characteristics of the place through repeated use and promoting children's participation in care and maintenance of the place; allows children to express themselves freely in creation and control of territories and special places; and protects the secrets and activities of children in these childhood places from harm.

(Chatterjee, 2005:17)

Whilst experiences in expansive natural habitats are valuable, especially for restoration, all children need access to everyday nature:

For children everywhere we should be providing regular opportunities for the everyday enjoyment of natural environments close to home – wild commonlands, gardens, ponds, city farms, schoolgrounds etc. …

(Hart, 1997:19)

In developing planned outdoor space to support natural play, the findings from this review lead to the following considerations:

- Recognising children's preferred sites for play, play provision should provide outdoor spaces with access to natural features and elements, greenery, bushes and trees, and accompanying natural 'loose parts'. Models of good practice in design and implementation of naturalistic playgrounds exist both internationally and within the UK.
- The space should maximise children's opportunity to move in a variety of different ways (Moore; 1989) and offer child-scale experiences of self-initiated play including adventure, risk-taking, rites of passage and exploration (Derr, 2002).
- Research indicates that 'settings that provide both varied forms of stimulation and subtle changes in that stimulation, similar to what is found in the natural world, are the most nourishing' (Olds, 2001:22). Alongside this, an environment which supports contrasts; light/dark; high/low; soft/hard, something/nothing; order/mystery; a range of features that provide ongoing interest is likely to provide strong emotional stimuli to support diverse play experiences.
- Natural spaces offer a greater disassociation from adult agendas than those from largely fabricated materials. There may be times when adults may prompt the child as a way of opening up possibilities, but there should always exist play opportunities that children can discover or realise on their own.

- There should be the opportunity for children to find or create their own special spaces with minimum adult involvement or intervention. Thus, places should contain options for privacy and the opportunity to meet together, nooks and crannies and contrasting spaces, opportunities to construct dens and shelters, etc., all of which combine to establish a sense of freedom and ownership.
- Planned play provision should provide a transitional space that allows for the needs of children changing over space and time, and not as a contested site where the use of space is fought for against the wishes and desires of those who hold adult power.

Environmental play provision

Environmental play provision is widespread and growing within the UK and has a significant role in meeting children's needs for engaging and freely chosen play experiences in natural environments. However, the provision is currently fragmented both geographically and in terms of sustainability. Continuity of funding is vital to maintain the long-term viability of individual projects and help develop a more comprehensive provision for children to access high quality environmental play. Development of appropriate, accessible training in environmental playwork is also crucial to ensure that the role of facilitating environmental play is adopted across the workforce, not just by 'specialists'.

Partnership working across a number of different sectors, in particular playwork and environmental education, has been – and continues to be – a strong point in environmental play provision. Arguably there is a need for a network of environmental play providers to be extended to a national level, or even UK-wide, perhaps following the model of the National Federation of City Farms. The role of such a network could include:

- raising the profile of environmental play
- sharing ideas, best practice and resources
- tackling common issues collectively, e.g. insurance
- training and professional development
- supporting new projects and initiatives.

Adams, J. (2003) 'In Defence of Bad Luck'. Spiked essays available online at: www.spiked-online.co.uk/Articles/00000006E02C.htm (accessed 27/05/06).

Aitken, S. (1994) *Putting Children in Their Place*. Washington: Edwards Bros.

Aitken, S. (2001) *Geographies of Young People*. London: Routledge.

Aitken, S. and Herman, T. (1997) 'Gender, Power and Crib Geography: transitional spaces and potential places', *Gender, Place and Culture*, 4(1), 63–88.

Altman I. and Wohwill, J. (eds) (1978) *Children and the Environment*. New York: Plenum Press.

Altman, I. and Low, S. (eds) (1992) *Place Attachment*. New York: Plenum Press.

Appleton, J. (1975) *The Experience of Landscape*. New York: Wiley.

Armitage, M. (2004) 'Hide and Seek – Where do children spend their time after school?' A paper for the Child in the City Conference, London.

Armstrong, N. (1993) 'Independent mobility and children's physical development', in Hillman, M. (ed.) *Children, Transport and the Quality of Life*. London: Policy Studies Institute.

Bachelard, G. (1969) *The Poetics of Reverie*. Boston: Beacon Press.

Barnardo's and Transport (2000) *Stop, Look and Listen: Children talk about traffic*. Ilford: Barnado's.

Baskin, Y. (1997) *The Work of Nature: How the diversity of life sustains us*. Washington: Island Press.

Bateson, P. and Martin, P. (1999) *Design for a Life*. London: Jonathan Cape.

Beck, U. (1992) *Risk Society: Towards a new modernity*. London: Sage.

Bell, J. (2005) *Doing Your Research Project*. Maidenhead: Open University Press.

Bingley, A. and Milligan, C. (2004) 'Climbing Trees and Building Dens: Mental health and well-being in young adults and the long-term experience of childhood play experiences', Institute for Health Research, Lancaster University, available on-line at: http://www.lancs.ac.uk/fass/ihr/publications/amandabingley/climbing_trees_and_building_dens.pdf (accessed 24/06/06).

Bixler, R., Floyd, M. and Hammitt, W. (2002) 'Environmental Socialization: Quantitative tests of the childhood play hypothesis', *Environment and Behaviour*, Vol. 34, no. 6, 795–818.

Blasi, C. and Bjorklund, D. (2003) 'Evolutionary Development Psychology: A new tool for better understanding human ontogeny', *Human Development*, 46, 259–281.

Blatchford, P. (1998) 'The State of Play in Schools', *Child Psychology and Psychiatry Review*, Vol. 3, no. 2, 58–67.

Blinkert, B. (2004) 'Quality of the City for Children: Chaos and order', *Children, Youth and Environments*, Vol. 14(2), 99–112.

BMA (2005) *Preventing Childhood Obesity*. London: BMA.

Bogin, B. (1998) 'Evolutionary and Biological Aspects of Childhood', Panter-Brick, C. (ed.) *Biosocial Perspectives on Childhood*. Cambridge: Cambridge University Press.

Boseley, S. (2005) 'Doctors urge action on "diabesity"', *Guardian*, 23/07/05.

Brown, F. (ed.) (2003) *Playwork: Theory and practice*. Buckingham: Open University Press.

Bruner, J., Jolly, A. and Sylva, K. (eds) (1976) *Play – its Role in Development and Evolution*. Harmondsworth: Penguin.

Burghardt, G. (2005) *The Genesis of Animal Play: Testing the limits*. Cambridge: MIT Press.

Burke, C. (2005) 'Play in Focus: Children researching their own spaces and places for play', *Children, Youth and Environments*, Vol. 15(1), 27–53.

CABE (2002) 'Paving the Way: How we achieve clean safe and attractive streets', available online at: www.cabe.org.uk/AssetLibrary/2025.pdf (accessed 27/05/06).

CABE (2004) 'Involving Young People in the Design and Care of Urban Spaces', available online at: www.cabe.org.uk/AssetLibrary/2103.pdf (accessed 28/05/06).

CABE (2005) *Start with Park: Creating sustainable urban green spaces in areas of housing growth and renewal*. London: CABE.

Canter, D. (1977) *The Psychology of Space*. London: The Architectural Press.

Capra, F. (1997) *The Web of Life*. London: Flamingo.

Capra, F. (2003) *The Hidden Connections*. London: Flamingo.

Carson, R. (1965) *The Sense of Wonder*. New York: Harper and Row. Cited in Lear, L. (1999) *Lost Woods*. Boston: Beacon.

Carter, R. (1998) *Mapping the Mind*. London: Phoenix.

Carver, S., Evans, A. and Fritz, S. (2002) 'Wilderness Attribute Mapping in the United Kingdom', *International Journal of Wilderness*, Vol. 8(1), 24–29.

Chapeniuk, R. (1995) 'Childhood Foraging as a Means of Acquiring Competent Human Cognition about Biodiversity', *Environment and Behaviour*, 27(4), 490–512.

Chatterjee, S. (2003) 'Exploring the Relationship between Children's Participation in Design and Affordance of Behaviour Settings', Research proposal DDN 701 Research Methods in Design, available online at: ncsudesign.org/content/baran/ddn701/chatterjee_ddn701_final.pdf (accessed 29/05/06).

Chatterjee, S. (2005) 'Children's Friendship with Place: A conceptual inquiry', *Children, Youth and Environments*, 15(1), 1–26.

Chawla, L. (1986) 'The Ecology of Environmental Memory', *Children's Environments Quarterly*, Vol. 3, no. 4, 34–42.

Chawla, L. (1990) 'Ecstatic Places', *Children's Environments Quarterly*, Vol. 7(4), 18–23.

Chawla, L. (1992) 'Childhood Place Attachments', in Altman, I. and Low, S. (eds) *Place Attachment*. New York: Plenum Press.

Chawla, L. (1994) *In the First Country of Places*. Albany, New York State: University of New York Press.

Chawla, L. (2002) 'Spots of Time: Manifold ways of being in nature in childhood', in Kahn, P. and Kellert, S. (eds) *Children and Nature*. Cambridge: MIT Press.

Children's Play Council (1998) *The New Charter for Children's Play*. London: National Children's Bureau.

Children's Play Council (2006) *Planning for Play: Guidance on the development and implementation of a local play strategy*. National Children's Bureau/Big Lottery Fund.

Children's Society/Children's Play Council (2001) *Play Space Survey*. Summary of results available online at: www.the-childrenssociety.org.uk/media/pdf/info/Play_Space_Survey.pdf (accessed 20/05/06).

Children's Society/Children's Play Council (2003) *Playday Survey*. Summary of results available online at: www.the-childrens-society.org.uk/media/pdf/media/Grumpy_Grown_Ups_Summary.pdf (accessed 24/06/06).

Childress, H. (2004) 'Teenagers, Territory and the Appropriation of Space', *Childhood*, Vol. 11(2), 195–205.

Chilton, T. (2003) 'Adventure playgrounds in the twenty-first century', in Brown, F. (ed.) *Playwork: Theory and practice*. Buckingham: Open University Press.

Chilton-Pearce, J. (1992) *Magical Child*. New York: Plume.

Chipeniuk, R. (1995) 'Childhood Foraging as a Means of Acquiring Competent Human Cognition about Biodiversity', *Environment and Behaviour*, Vol. 27, 490–512.

Christensen, P. (2002) 'Why More "Quality Time" is not on the Top of Children's Lists: The qualities of time for children', *Children and Society*, Vol. 16(2), 77–88.

Christensen, P. and O'Brien, M. (eds) (2003) *Children in the City*. London: RoutledgeFalmer.

Chugani, H., Behan, M., Muzik, O., Juhasz, C., Nagy, F. and Chugani, C. (2001) 'Local Brain Functional Activity Following Early Deprivation: A study of Postinstitutionlised Romanian Orphans', *Neuroimage*, Vol. 14, 1290–1301.

Clements, R. (2004) 'An Investigation of the State of Outdoor Play', *Contemporary Issues in Early Childhood*, Vol. 5(1): 68–80.

Cobb, E. (1977) *The Ecology of Imagination in Childhood*. New York: Columbia University Press.

Cohen, S. (1994) 'Children and the Environment: Aesthetic learning', *Childhood Education*, Vol. 70(5), 302–305.

Collins, D. and Kearns, R. (2001) 'Under Curfew and under Siege? Legal Geographies of Young People', *Geoforum*, 32, 389–403.

Connick-Smith, N. and Gutman, M. (2004) 'Children and Youth in Public', *Childhood*, Vol. 11(2), 131–141.

Conway, M., Hughes, B., Sturrock, G. (2004) *A New Perspective for Playwork*. Sheffield: Ludemos Press.

Cornell, E., Hadley, D., Sterling, T., Chan, M. and Boechler, P. (2001) 'Adventure as a Stimulus for Cognitive Development', *Journal of Environmental Psychology* 21, 219–231.

Cranwell, K. (2003) 'Towards Playwork: An historical introduction to children's out-of-school play organisations in London (1860–1940)', in Brown, F. (ed.) *Playwork: theory and practice*. Buckingham: Open University Press.

Cullen, G. (1961) *The Concise Townscape*. New York: Van Nostrand Rhienhold. Cited in Kaplan, R. and Kaplan, S. (1989) *The Experience of Nature: A psychological perspective*. New York: Cambridge.

Cunningham, C. and Jones, M. (1991) 'Girls and Boys Come out to Play: Play, gender and urban planning', *Landscape Australia*, Vol. 4, 305–311. Cited in Karsten, L. (2003) 'Children's Use of Public Space: The gendered world of the playground', *Childhood*, Vol. 10(4), 457–473.

Damasio, A. (1994) *Descartes Error. Emotion, reason and the human brain*. New York: HarperCollins.

Damasio, A. (2003) *Looking For Spinoza*. London: William Heinemann.

Derr, V. (2002) 'Children's Sense of Place in Northern New Mexico', *Journal of Environmental Psychology* 22, 125–137.

Deleuze, G. and Guattari, F. (1988) *A Thousand Plateaus*. London: Continuum.

Dietz, W. (2001) 'The Obesity Epidemic in Young Children', *British Medical Journal*, Vol. 322, 313–314.

Dixey, R. (1999) 'Keeping Children Safe: The effect on parent's daily lives and psychological well-being', *Journal of Health Psychology*, Vol. 4(1), 45–57.

Doll, B. (1996) 'Children Without Friends: Implications for policy and practice', *The School Psychology Review*, 25(2), 165–183 cited in Chatterjeee, S. (2005) 'Children's Friendship With Place: A conceptual inquiry', in *Children, Youth and Environments*, 15(1), 1–26.

Douglas, I. (2005) 'Urban Greenspace and Mental Health', review paper prepared for UK MAB Urban Forum.

Dovey, K. (1990) 'Refuge and Imagination: Places of Peace. Childhood', *Children's Environments Quarterly*, 7(4), 13–17.

DTLR (2002) 'Green Spaces, Better Places', final report of the Urban Green Spaces Task Force, available online at: www.odpm.gov.uk/pub/706/GreenspacesbetterplacesfinalreportPDF1488Kb_id11 27706.pdf (accessed 30/05/06).

Dunn, K. and Moore, M. (2005) 'Developing Accessible Play Space in the UK: A social model approach', *Children, Youth and Environments*, Vol. 15(1), 331–353.

Earthkids (1989) *I Know Someone who's Afraid of Sunflowers: A guide to good practice in the provision of environmental play*. Birmingham: The Urban Wildlife Trust.

Ebbeling, C., Pawlak, D. and Ludwig, D. (2002) 'Childhood Obesity; public health crisis, common sense cure', *Lancet*, 360, 473–482.

Elsley, S. (2004) 'Children's Experience of Public Space', *Childhood and Society*, Vol. 18, 155–164.

Ennew, J. (1994) 'Time for Children or Time for Adults', in Quortrop, J. and others (eds) *Childhood Matters! Social theory, practice and politics*. Aldershot: Avebury Press.

Factor, J. (2004) 'Tree Stumps, Manhole Covers and Rubbish Tins: The invisible play lines of a primary school playground', *Childhood*, Vol. 11(2), 142–154.

Fagen, R. (1981) *Animal Play Behaviour*. New York: Oxford University Press. Cited in Sutton-Smith, B. (1997) *The Ambiguity of Play*. Cambridge: Harvard University Press.

Fjortoft, I. (2001) 'The Natural Environment as Playground for Children: The impact of outdoor play activities in pre-primary school children', *Environmental Education*, Vol. 29(2), 111–117.

Fjortoft, I. (2004) 'Landscape and Play: The effects of natural environments on children's play and motor development', *Children, Youth and Environments*, 14(2), 21–44.

Fjortoft, I. and Sageie, J. (2000) 'The Natural Environment as a Playground for Children', *Landscape and Urban Planning*, 48, 83–97.

Franklin, T. and Connolly, P. (2003) 'Streets of Fear or Streets of Fun? Living Streets', available online at: www.livingstreets.org.uk/download/71-Streets-of-Fear-or-Streets-of-Fun-pamphlet.pdf (accessed 18/05/06).

Freeman, C. (1995) 'Planning and Play: Creating greener environments', *Children's Environments*, Vol. 12(3), 164–176.

Frost, J. (1992) *Play and playscapes*. Albany: Delmar.

Frost, J. (2006) 'The Dissolution of Children's Outdoor Play: Causes and consequences', presentation to 'The Value Of Play'; a forum on risk, recreation and children's health, 31 May 2006, available online at: cgood.org/assets/attachments/Frost_-_Common_Good_-_FINAL.pdf (accessed 28/06/06).

Frumkin, H. (2001) 'Beyond Toxicity: Human health and the natural environment', *American Journal of Preventative Medicine*, 20(3), 232–240.

Furedi, F. (2002) *The Culture of Fear*. London: Cassell.

Gabarino, J. (1985) 'Habitats for Children: An ecological perspective', in Wohlwill, J. and Van Vliet, W. (eds) *Habitats for Children*. New Jersey: Lawrence Erlbaum.

Gagen, E. (2000) 'Playing the Part: Performing gender in America's playgrounds', in Holloway, S. and Valentine, G. (eds) *Children's Geographies*. London: Routledge.

Gaster, S. (1991) 'Urban Children's Access to their Neighbourhood', *Environment and Behaviour*, Vol. 23(1), 70–85.

Gebser, J. (1985) *The Ever-Present Origin*. Athens: Ohio University Press. Cited in Chawla, L. (2002) 'Spots of Time: Manifold ways of being in nature in childhood', in Kahn, P. and Kellert, S. (eds) *Children and Nature*. Cambridge: MIT Press.

Gibson, J. (1986) *The Ecological Approach to Visual Perception*. New Jersey: Laurence Erlbaum.

Giddings, R. and Yarwood, R. (2005) 'Growing Up, Going Out and Growing Out of the Countryside: Childhood experiences in rural England', in *Children's Geographies*, Vol. 3(91), 101–114.

Gill, T. (2005) 'Let our Children Roam Free', *The Ecologist*, available online at: www.theecologist.org/archive_detail.asp?content_id=481 (accessed 16/05/06).

Gill, T. (2006) 'Homes Zones in the UK: History, policy and impact on children and youth', *Children, Youth and Environments*, Vol. 16(1), 90–103.

Gill, T. (2006) 'Growing adventure: Final report to the Forestry Commission', available online: www.forestry.gov.uk/england-play (accessed 30/05/06).

Ginsberg, O. (2000) 'Adventure Playgrounds and City Farms in Europe and What They Contribute to Sustainable Urban Development', presentation to Anima21 Adventure Playgrounds and City Farms Conference, Berlin, 1999, available online at: http://www.bdja.org/oli/index.html (accessed 25/06/06).

Grayling, T., Hallam, K., Graham, D., Anderson, R. and Glaister, S. (2002) *Streets ahead*. London: Institute for Public Policy Research.

Guiliani, M. and Feldman, R. (1993) 'Place Attachment in a Developmental and Cultural Context', *Journal of Environmental Psychology*, 13, 267–274. Cited in Manzo, L. (2003) 'Beyond House and Haven: toward a revisioning of emotional relationships with places', *Journal of Environmental Psychology*, 23, 47–61.

Gullone, E. (2000) 'The Biophilia Hypothesis and Life in the 21st Century: Increasing mental health or increasing pathology?', *Journal of Happiness Studies*, Vol. 1, 293–321.

Gustafson, P. (2001) 'Meanings of Place: Everyday experience and theoretical conceptualisations', *Journal of Environmental Psychology*, 21, 5–16.

Hallden, G. (2003) 'Children's Views of Family, Home and House', in Christensen, P. and O'Brien, M. (eds) *Children in the City*. London: RoutledgeFalmer.

Hansen, E.B. (1999) 'Løkke og lag. Hvordan barn trener i dag? Norges i dretts forbund og Olympiske komite', cited in Fjortoft, I. (2001) 'The Natural Environment as Playground for Children: The impact of outdoor play activities in pre-primary school children', *Environmental Education*, Vol. 29(2), 111–117.

Harden, J. (2000) 'There's No Place Like Home', *Childhood*, Vol. 7(1), 43–59.

Harrop, P. (2006) 'Rope Swings, Dens, Tree Houses and Fires. Forestry Commission', available online at: www.forestry.gov.uk/england-play (accessed 30/05/06).

Hart, R. (1979) *Children's Experience of Place*. New York: Irvington.

Hart, R. (1997) *Children's Participation in Sustainable Development*. London: Earthscan.

Hart, R. (2004) 'The Worlds We Make for Children: Thinking critically of space, place and the material world in children's learning',

Kinsey Dialogue Series, available online at:
www.umass.edu/cie/kinsey/index.htm#hart (accessed 27/06/06).

Hartig, T., Mang, M. and Evans, G. (1991) 'Restorative Effects of
Natural Environment Experiences', *Environment and Behaviour*,
Vol. 23(1), 3–26.

Hartrup, W. (1991) 'Having Friends, Making Friends, and Keeping
Friends: Relationships as educational contexts', *Early Report*, 19,
1–4, cited in Chatterjee, S. (2005) 'Children's Friendship with Place:
A conceptual inquiry', *Children, Youth and Environments*, 15(1), 1–26.

Hay, R. (1998) 'Sense of Place in Developmental Context', *Journal of
Environmental Psychology*, 18, 5–29.

Heft, H. (1988) 'Affordances of Children's Environments', *Children's
Environments Quarterly*, 5(3), 29–37. Cited in Kytta, M. (2004) 'The
Extent of Children's Independent mobility and the Number of
Actualized Affordances as Criteria for Child-Friendly
Environments', *Journal of Environmental Psychology*, 24, 179–198.

Heft, H. (1989) 'Affordances and the Body: An international analysis
of Gibson's ecological approach to visual perception', *Journal for
the Theory of Social Behaviour*, 19(1), 1–30.

Herrington, S. and Studtmann, K. (1998) 'Landscape Interventions:
New directions for the design of children's outdoor play
environments', *Landscape and Urban Planning*, Vol. 42, 191–205.

Hillman, M., Adams, J. and Whitelegg, J. (1990) *One False Move:
A study of children's independent mobility*. London: Policy Studies
Institute.

Hillman, M. and Adams, J. (1992) 'Children's Freedom and Safety',
Children's Environments, Vol. 9(2), 12–33.

Hocking, G. and Thomas, G. (2003) 'Other People's Children: Why their
quality of life is our concern'. London: Demos [online] available
from: www.demos.co.uk/catalogue/otherpeopleschildren2
(accessed 21/05/06).

Hodgson, J. (1988) *The National Trust for Aesthetic Education*,
London. Cited in Cohen, S. (1996) 'Children and the Environment:
aesthetic learning', *Childhood Education*, Vol. 70(5), 302–305.

Holland, P. (2003) *We Don't Play with Guns Here*. Maidenhead: Open
University Press.

Holloway, S. and Valentine, G. (eds) (2000) *Children's Geographies*.
London: Routledge.

Houston, L., Worthington, R. and Harrop, P. (2006) 'Design Guidance
for Play Spaces', Forestry Commission, available online:
www.forestry.gov.uk/englandplay (accessed 30/05/06).

Hughes, B. (1996) *Play Environments: A question of quality*. London: Playlink.

Hughes, B. (2001) *Evolutionary Playwork and Reflective Analytical Practice*. London: Routledge.

Hughes, B. (2002) *A Taxonomy of Play Types*. London: Playlink.

Huttenmoser, M. (1995) 'Children and Their Living Surroundings', *Children's Environments*, 12(4), 1–17.

Huttenmoser, M. and Degen-Zimmerman, D. (1995) *Lebensraume fur Kinder*. Maria Meierhofer-Institut fur das kind: Zurich.

ILAM (2001) 'Response to the NPFA Six Acre Standard', available online at: www.ilam.co.uk/pol-01-09.asp (accessed 31/05/06).

James, W. (1892) *Psychology: The briefer course*. New York: Henry Holt. Cited in Kaplan, S. (2002) 'Some Hidden Benefits of the Urban Forest', conference paper, IUFRO European Regional Conference, Copenhagen.

Johnson, L.M. (2004) 'American Playgrounds and Schoolyards – A time for change', paper presented to Open Space, People Space Conference, available online at: www.openspace.eca.ac.uk/conference/proceedings/summary/Macmillan.htm (accessed 22/05/06).

Johnston, M. (2004) 'Clinical Disorders of Brain Plasticity', *Brain and Development*, Vol. 26, 73–80.

Jones, O. (1997) 'Little Figures, Big Shadows: Country childhood stories', in Cloke, P. and Little, J. (eds) *Contested Countryside Cultures*. London: Routledge.

Jones, O. (2000) 'Melting Geography: Purity, disorder, childhood and space', in Holloway, S. and Valentine, G. (eds) *Children's Geographies*. London: Routledge.

Kahn, P. (1999) *The Human Relationship with Nature*. Cambridge: MIT Press.

Kahn, P. and Kellert, S. (eds) (2002) *Children and Nature*. Cambridge: MIT Press.

Kaplan, R. and Kaplan, S. (1989) *The Experience of Nature: A psychological perspective*. New York: Cambridge.

Kaplan, S. (1992) 'Environmental Preferences in a Knowledge-Seeking, Knowledge-Using Organism', in Barkow, J., Cosmides, L. and Tooby, J. (eds) *The Adapted Mind: Evolutionary psychology and the generation of culture*. New York: Oxford University Press.

Kaplan, S. (1995) 'The Restorative Benefits of Nature: Toward an integrative framework', *Journal of Environmental Psychology*, 15, 169–182.

Kaplan, S. (2001) 'Meditation, Restoration and the Management of Mental Fatigue', *Environment and Behaviour*, Vol. 33(4), 480–506.

Kaplan, S. (2002) 'Some Hidden Benefits of the Urban Forest', conference paper, IUFRO European Regional Conference, Copenhagen. Paper presented on 27/08/02.

Karsten, L. (2003) 'Children's Use of Public Space: The gendered world of the playground', *Childhood*, Vol. 10(4), 457–473.

Karsten, L. (2005) 'It All Used to be Better? Different generations on continuity and change in urban children's daily use of space', *Children's Geographies*, Vol. 3(3), 275–290.

Karsten, L. and Van Vliet, W. (2006) 'Increasing Children's Freedom of Movement: Introduction', *Children, Youth and Environments*, Vol. 16(1), 69–73.

Katcher, A. (2002) 'Animals in Therapeutic Education: Guides into the liminal state', in Kahn, P. and Kellert, S. (eds) *Children and Nature*. Cambridge: MIT Press.

Kellert, S. (1996) *The Value of Life: Biological diversity and human society*. Washington DC: Island Press.

Kellert, S. (1997) *Kinship to Mastery: Biophilia in human evolution and development*. Washington DC: Island Press.

Kellert, S. (2002) 'Experiencing Nature: Affective, cognitive, and evaluative development in children', in Kahn, P. and Kellert, S. (eds) *Children and Nature*. Cambridge: MIT Press.

Kellert, S. and Wilson, E.O. (eds) (1993) *The Biophilia Hypothesis*. Washington: Island Press.

Kelso, P. (2002) 'Health Problems Growing after Decades of Neglect on the Playing Fields of Britain', *Guardian*, 16/12/02.

King, A. (1996) 'Spirituality: Transformation and metamorphosis', *Religion*, Vol. 26, 343–351.

Kirby, M. (1989) 'Nature as Refuge', *Children's Environments Quarterly* 6.1, 7–12. Cited in Nabhan, G. and Trimble, S. (1994) *The Geography of Childhood*. Boston: Beacon Press.

Kjorholt, A. (2003) 'Creating a Place to Belong: Girls and boys hut building as a site for understanding discourses on childhood and generational issues on a Norwegian community', *Children's Geographies*, Vol. 1(1), 261–279.

Korpela, K. and Hartig, T. (1996) 'Restorative Qualities of Favourite Places', *Journal of Environmental Psychology*, 16, 221–223.

Korpela, K., Kytta, M. and Hartig, T. (2002) 'Restorative Experience, Self-Regulation and Children's Special Place Preferences', *Journal of Environmental Psychology*, 22, 387–398.

Kuo, F. and Sullivan, W. (2001) 'Aggression and Violence in the Inner City: Effects of environment via mental fatigue', *Environment and Behaviour*, Vol. 33(4), 543–571.

Kuo, F., Sullivan, W. and DePooter, S. (2004) 'The Fruit of Urban Nature: Vital Neighbourhood Spaces', *Environment and Behaviour*, Vol. 36(5), 678–700.

Kylin, M. (2003) 'Children's Dens', *Children, Youth and Environments*, 13(1), Spring.

Kytta, M. (2002) 'Affordances of Children's Environments in the Context of Cities, Small Towns, Suburbs and Rural Villages in Finland and Belarus', *Journal of Environmental Psychology*, 22, 109–123.

Kytta, M. (2004) 'The Extent of Children's Independent Mobility and the Number of Actualized Affordances as Criteria for Child-Friendly Environments', *Journal of Environmental Psychology*, 24, 179–198.

Lear, L. (1999) *Lost Woods*. Boston: Beacon.

Lester, S. (2005) PL306 Workbook: *Playing Out*. Gloucester: University of Gloucestershire.

Lester, S. (2006) PL302 Workbook: *Play Cultures and Children's Communities*. Gloucester: University of Gloucestershire.

Lewontin, R. (2000) *The Triple Helix*. Cambridge: Harvard University Press.

Lohr, V. and Pearson-Mims, C. (2005) 'Children's Active and Passive Interactions with Plants Influence Their Attitudes and Actions Towards Trees and Gardening as Adults', *Horticultural Technology*, Vol. 15(3), 472–476.

Louv, R. (1992) *Childhood's Future*. Anchor Press. Cited in Sobel, D. (1995) 'Beyond Ecophobia: Reclaiming the heart in nature education', available online at: www.arts.envirolink.org/arts_and_education/DavidSobel1.html (accessed 14/05/06).

Louv, R. (2005) *Last Child in the Woods: Saving our children from Nature-Deficit Disorder*. Chapel Hill: Algonquin.

Lupton, D. (1999) *Risk*. London: Routledge.

Maan, N. (2005) 'The Delivery of Environmental Play Projects by the Better Play Funded Organisations', Barnardo's, available online at: www.barnardos.org.uk/briefing_paper_4_-_environmental_play_-.pdf (accessed 28/05/06).

Mackett, R. and Paskins, J. (2004) 'Increasing Children's Volume of Physical Activity Through Walk and Play', contribution to the Dept. of Culture, Media and Sport and Dept. of Health consultation on 'Choosing Health, Choosing Activity'. Available online at: www.cts.ucl.ac.uk/research/chcaruse/Choose.pdf (accessed 28/05/06).

Malone, K. (2002) 'Street life: Youth, culture and competing uses of public space', *Environment and Urbanisation*, Vol. 14, no. 2, 157–168.

Manzo, L. (2003) 'Beyond House and Haven: Toward a revisioning of emotional relationships with places', *Journal of Environmental Psychology*, 23, 47–61.

Massey, D. (1994) *Space, Place and Gender*. Cambridge: Polity.

Matthews, H. (1992) *Making Sense of Place*. Hemel Hempstead: Harvester Wheatsheaf.

Matthews, H. (1995) 'Living on the Edge: Children as "outsiders"', *Tijdschrift voor Economische en Sociale Geograffe*, Vol. 86, 456–466.

Matthews, H., Taylor, M., Sherwood, K., Tucker, F. and Limb, M. (2000a) 'Growing Up in the Countryside: Children and the rural idyll', *Journal of Rural Studiès*, Vol. 18, 193–207.

Matthews, H., Limb, M. and Taylor, M. (2000b) 'The "Street" as Thirdspace', Holloway, S. and Valentine, G. (eds) (2000) *Children's Geographies*. London: Routledge.

Mattson, K. (2002) 'Children's (In)dependent Mobility and Parents Chauffering in the Town and Countryside', *Tijdschrift voor Economische en Sociale Geograffe*, Vol. 93, no. 4, 443–453.

Maudsley, M.J. (ed.) (2005) *Playing on the Wildside*. Cheltenham: Playwork Partnerships.

Maudsley M.J. (2006) 'Playing Naturally: Celebrating the playfulness of nature'. *Play Today* issue 53, available online at: www.ncb.org.uk/Page.asp?sve=912 (accessed 03/07/06).

Mayall, B. and Hood, S. (2001) 'Breaking Barriers: Provision and participation in an out-of-school centre', *Children and Society*, Vol. 15, 70–81.

Mayall, B. (2002) *Towards a Sociology for Childhood*. Buckingham: Open University Press.

McKendrick, J., Bradford, M. and Fielder, A. (2000) 'Kid Customer? Commercialisation of playspace and the commodification of childhood', *Childhood*, Vol. 7(3), 259–314.

McNeish, D. (2005) 'Stop, Look and Listen: How real is our commitment to evidence based policy?', *Children's Geographies*, Vol. 3(1), 115–118.

McNeish, D. and Roberts, H. (1995) *Playing it Safe*. London: Barnardo's.

Mental Health Foundation (1999) *Bright Futures: Promoting children and young people's mental health*. London: Mental Health Foundation.

Mergan, B. (2003) 'Children and Nature in History', *Environmental History*, Vol. 8(4).

Moore, R. (1986) *Childhood's Domain*. London: Croom Helm.

Moore, R. (1987) 'Streets as Playgrounds', Moudon, A. (ed) *Public Streets for Public Use*. New York: Van Nostrand Rienhold.

Moore, R. (1989) 'Playgrounds at the Crossroads', in Altman, I. and Zube, E. 'Public Places and Spaces', in *Human Behaviour and the Environment*, Vol. 10. New York: Plenum Press.

Moore, R. (1997) 'The Need for Nature: A childhood right', *Social Justice*, Vol. 24(3), 203–213.

Moore, R. and Cosco, N. (2000) 'Developing an Earthbound Culture Through Design of Childhood Habitats', Natural Learning Organisation, available online at: www.naturalearning.org/earthboundpaper.html (accessed 24/05/06).

Moore, R. and Wong, H. (1997) *Natural Learning: Creating Environments for Rediscovering Nature's Way of Teaching*. Berkeley: MIG Communications.

Moore, R. and Young, D. (1978) 'Childhood Outdoors: Towards a social ecology of the landscape', in Altman, I. and Wohwill, J. (eds) *Children and the Environment*. New York: Plenum Press.

Morris, N. (2003) 'Black and Minority Ethnic Groups and Public Open Space', Edinburgh: OPENspace, available online at: www.openspace.eca.ac.uk/pdf/BlackMinorityIndLitRev.pdf (accessed 14/05/06).

Moss, P. and Petrie, P. (2002) *From Children's Services to Children's Spaces: Public policy, children and childhood*. London: RoutledgeFalmer.

Myers, O. and Saunders, C. (2002) 'Animals as Links towards Developing Caring Relationships with the Natural World', in Kahn, P. and Kellert, S. (eds) *Children and Nature*. Cambridge: MIT Press.

National Foundation for Educational Research (2004) 'A Research Review of Outdoor Learning', available online at: www.nfer.ac.uk (accessed 28/06/06).

Nabhan, G. and Trimble, S. (1994) *The Geography of Childhood*. Boston: Beacon Press.

Naess, A. (1973) 'The Shallow and the Deep, Long-Range Ecology Movement: A summary', *Inquiry*, Vol. 16, 95–100.

Nairn, K., Panelli, R. and McCormack, J. (2003) 'Destabilising Dualisms: Young people's experiences of rural and urban environments', *Childhood*, Vol. 10(1), 9–42.

Nebelong, H. (2002) 'Designs on Play', speech to Playlink/Portsmouth City Council conference, available online at: www.freeplaynetwork.org.uk/design/nebelong.htm (accessed 18/05/06).

Nicholson, S. (1971) 'How Not to Cheat Children: The theory of loose parts', *Landscape Architecture*, 62(1), 30–35.

Noren-Bjorn, E. (1982) *The Impossible Playground*. New York: Leisure Press.

NPFA, Children's Play Council and PLAYLINK (2000) *Best Play: What play provision should do for children*. London: NPFA.

NPFA (2001) *The Six-Acre Standard: Minimum standards for outdoor playing space*. London: NPFA.

O'Brien, M., Jones, D. and Rustin, M. (2000) 'Children's Independent Spatial Mobility in the Public Realm', *Childhood*, Vol. 7(3), 257–277.

Olds, A.R. (2001) *Child Care Design Guide*. New York: McGraw-Hill.

OPENspace (2006a) 'Wild Adventure Space: Literature review prepared for the Countryside Agency, English Nature and Rural Development Service', available online at: www.openspace.eca.ac.uk/WildAdventureSpace.htm (accessed 28/05/06).

OPENspace (2006b) 'Wild Adventure Space: Project review prepared for the Countryside Agency, English Nature and Rural Development Service', available online at: www.openspace.eca.ac.uk/WildAdventureSpace.htm (accessed 28/05/06).

Orians, G. and Heerwagen, J. (1992) 'Evolved Responses to Landscapes', in Barkow, J., Cosmides, L. and Tooby, J. (eds) *The Adapted Mind: Evolutionary psychology and the generation of culture*. New York: Oxford University Press.

Orians, G. and Heerwagen, J. (2002) 'The Ecological World of Children', in Kahn, P. and Kellert, S. (eds) *Children and Nature*. Cambridge: MIT Press.

Orr, D. (2002) 'Political Economy and the Ecology of Childhood', in Kahn, P. and Kellert, S. (eds) *Children and Nature*. Cambridge: MIT Press.

Ota, C., Erricker, C. and Erricker, J. (1997) 'The Secrets of the Playground', *Pastoral Care*, December. 19–24.

Oyama, S. (2000) *Evolution's Eye. A systems view of the biology-culture divide*. London: Duke University Press.

Percy-Smith, B. (2002) 'Contested Worlds: Constraints and opportunities in city and suburban environments in an English midlands city', in Chawla, L. (ed.) *Growing Up in an Urbanising World*. London: Earthscan.

Persil (2005) 'The Positively Dirty Report', available from: www.dirtisgood.co.uk (accessed 03/07/06).

Peterson, J. (1985) 'The Adventure Playground in Denmark', in Frost, J. and Sunderlin, S. (eds) *When Children Play*. Wheaton: Association for Childhood Education International. Cited in Moore, R. (1989)

'Playgrounds at the Crossroads', in Altman, I. and Zube, E. (1989) 'Public Places and Spaces', *Human Behaviour and the Environment*, Vol. 10. New York: Plenum Press.

Philo, C (1992) 'Neglected Rural Geographies: A review', *Journal of Rural Studies*, Vol. 8, no. 2, 193–207.

Play Wales/PlayEd (2001) *The First Claim*. Cardiff: Play Wales.

Play Wales/PlayEd (2002) *The First Claim: Desirable processes*. Cardiff: Play Wales.

Play Wales (2005) *Playwork Principles*. Cardiff: Play Wales.

Playlink (2001) *Making Sense: Playwork in practice*. London: Playlink.

Pooley, C., Turnbull, G. and Adams, M. (2005) 'The Journey to School in Britain since the 1940s: Continuity and change', *Area*, Vol. 37(1), 43–53.

Power, T. (2000) *Play and Exploration in Children and Animals*. New Jersey: Erlbaum.

Prout, A. (2005) *The Future of Childhood*. Abingdon: RoutledgeFalmer.

Pyle, R. (2002) 'Eden as a Vacant Lot', Kahn, P. and Kellert, S. (eds) *Children and Nature*. Cambridge: MIT Press.

Rasmussen, K. (2004) 'Places for Children – Children's Places', *Childhood*, Vol. 11(2), 155–173.

Rasmussen, K. and Smidt, S. (2003) 'The Neighbourhood in the Children', in Christensen, P. and O'Brien, M. (eds) *Children in the City*. London: RoutledgeFalmer.

Relph, E. (1976) *Place and Placelessness*. London: Pion.

Rivkin, M (1995) *The Great Outdoors: Restoring children's right to play outside*. Washington: NAEYC.

Rivkin, M (1998) '"Happy Play in Grassy Places": The importance of the outdoor environment in Dewey's educational ideal', *Early Childhood Education Journal*, Vol. 25(3), 199–202.

Rivkin, M. (2000) 'Outdoor Experiences for Young Children', in *ERIC Digest EDO-RC-00-7*.

Rissotto, A. and Tonucci, F. (2002) 'Freedom of Movement and Environmental Knowledge in Elementary School Children', *Journal of Environmental Psychology*, 22, 65–77.

Rose, S. (1997) *Lifelines. Biology, Freedom, Determinism*. London: Penguin.

Rose, S. (2000) 'Escaping Evolutionary Psychology', in Rose, H. and Rose, S. (eds) *Alas, Poor Darwin*. London: Jonathan Cape.

Ross, N. (2004) '"That Tree Used to be Everything to Us": The importance of natural and unkempt environments to children', paper presented to Open Space, People Space Conference, available online at: www.openspace.eca.ac.uk/conference/ proceedings/summary/Ross.htm (accessed 14/05/06).

Rubenstein, D. (2002) 'On the Evolution of Juvenile Life-Styles in Mammals', in Pereira, M. and Fairbanks, L. (eds) *Juvenile Primates: Life history, development and behaviour*. Chicago: Chicago University Press. Cited in Prout, A. (2005) *The Future of Childhood*. Abingdon: RoutledgeFalmer.

Schroeder, H. and Lewis, C. (1991) 'Psychological Benefits and Costs of Urban Forests', proceedings of the Fifth National Urban Forest Conference, Los Angeles, Nov. 15–19.

Schultz, P., Shriver, C., Tabanico, J. and Khazian, A. (2004) 'Implicit Connections with Nature', Journal of Environmental Psychology, 24, 31–42.

Sebba, R. and Churchman, A. (1986) 'Schoolyard Design as an Expression of Educational Principles', *Children's Environments Quarterly*, 3(3), 70–76. Cited in Wilson, R. (2001) 'A Sense of Place', *EE News*, Vol. 18, no. 2, 2–7.

Sebba, R. (1991) 'The Landscapes of Childhood: The reflections of children's environment in adult memories and in children's attitudes', *Environment and Behaviour*, 23(4), 395–422.

Sheldrake, P. (2001) 'Human Identity and the Particularity of Place', *Spiritus*, 1(1), 43–64.

Sheriff, C. (2001) 'Nowhere Safe to Play: Safe kids at play campaign', paper presented to the 66th ROSPA Road Safety Congress, 12–14 March 2001.

Sibley, D. (1995) *Geographies of Exclusion*. London: Routledge

Skelton, T. (2000) 'Nothing to Do, Nowhere to Go?', in Holloway, S. and Valentine, G. (eds) *Children's Geographies*. London: Routledge.

Smith, F. and Barker, J. (2000) '"Out of School", in School: A social geography of out-of-school childcare', in Holloway, S. and Valentine, G. (eds) *Children's Geographies*. London: Routledge.

Smith, F. and Barker, J. (2001) 'Commodifying the Countryside: The impact of out-of-school care on rural landscapes of children's play', *Area*, Vol. 33(2), 169–176.

Sobel, D. (1990) 'A Place in the World: Adults memories of childhood's special places', *Children's Environments Quarterly*, 7(4), 5–12.

Sobel, D. (1993) *Children's Special Places*. Detroit: Wayne State University Press.

Sobel, D. (1995) 'Beyond Ecophobia: Reclaiming the heart in nature education', available online at: http://arts.envirolink.org/arts_and_ education/DavidSobel1.html (accessed 21/08/05).

Sobel, D. (1997) 'Map Making from the Inside Out: The cartography of childhood', Orion Afield, available online at: www.haven.net/deep/council/sobel.htm (accessed 29/05/06).

Splisbury, J. (2005) '"We Don't Really Get to go Out in the Front Yard": Children's home range and neighbourhood violence', Children's Geographies, Vol. 3(1), 79–99.

Stoecklin, V. (2000) 'Creating Playgrounds Kids Love'. White Hutchinson Leisure and Learning Group, available online at: www.whitehutchinson.com/children/articles/playgrndkidslove.shtml (accessed 21/05/06).

Sturrock, G. (2004) 'A New Playwork Perspective', Play Wales, available online at: www.playwales.org.uk/values/index.php?pg= supportingmaterials&lang=english (accessed 20/05/06).

Sturrock, G. and Else, P. (1998) 'The Playground as Therapeutic Space: Playwork as healing', proceedings of the IPA/USA Triennial National Conference, Play in a Changing Society: Research, design, application. London: IPA.

Sturrock, G., Russell, W. and Else, P. (2004) Towards Ludogogy: Parts 1, 2 and 3. The art of being and becoming through play. Sheffield: Ludemos.

Sutton-Smith, B. (1990) 'School Playground as Festival', Children's Environment's Quarterly, Vol. 7(2), 3–7. Cited in Nabhan, G. and Trimble, S. (1994) The Geography of Childhood. Boston: Beacon Press.

Sutton-Smith, B. (1997) The Ambiguity of Play. Cambridge: Harvard University Press.

Sutton-Smith, B. (1999) 'Evolving a Consilience of Play Definitions: Playfully', Play and Culture Studies 2, 239–256.

Sutton-Smith, B. (2002) 'Recapitulation Redressed', in Roopnarine, J. (ed.) Conceptual, Social-Cognitive, and Contextual Issues in the Fields of Play, Vol. 4. Westport: Ablex.

Sutton-Smith, B. (2003) 'Play as a Parody of Emotional Vulnerability', in Lytle, D. (ed.) Play and Culture Studies, Vol. 5. London: Praeger.

Tandy, C. (1999) 'Children's Diminishing Play Space: A study of intergenerational change in children's use of their neighbourhoods', Australian Geographical Studies, July 1999, 37(2), 154–164.

Taylor, A., Kuo, F. and Sullivan, W. (2001). 'Coping with ADD: The surprising connection to green play settings', Environment and Behaviour, Vol. 33(1), 54–77.

Taylor, B. (2001) 'Earth and Nature Based Spirituality: From deep ecology to radical environmentalism', Religion, Vol. 31, 175–193.

Thomas, G. and Thompson, G. (2004) A Child's Place: Why environment matters to children. London: Green Alliance/Demos, available online at: www.demos.co.uk/catalogue/achildsplacebook (accessed 14/05/06).

Thompson, J. and Philo, C. (2004) 'Playful Spaces? A social geography of children's play in Livingston, Scotland', *Children's Geographies*, Vol. 2, no. 1, 111–130.

Thompson, S. (2005) 'Territorialising the Primary School Playground: Deconstructing the geography of playtime', *Children's Geographies*, Vol. 3, no. 1, 63–78.

Titman, W. (1994) *Special Places, Special People: The hidden curriculum of school grounds*. London: WWF UK/Learning Through Landscapes.

Tranter, P. and Malone, K. (2004) 'Geographies of Environmental Learning: An exploration of the children's use of school grounds', *Children's Geographies*, Vol. 2, no. 1, 131–155.

Tuan, Y. (1974) *Topophilia: A study of environmental perception, attitudes and values*. New York: Columbia University Press.

Tuan, Y. (1978) 'Children and the Natural Environment', in Altman, I. and Wohwill, J. (eds) *Children and the Environment*. New York: Plenum Press.

Tuffin, R. (1996) 'There Ain't Much to Play, Most Things are for Adults', in *Children in an Urban Environment*. Centre for Institutional Studies: University of East London.

Ulrich, R. (1984) 'View Through a Window May Influence Recovery from Surgery', *Science*, 224, 420–421.

Ulrich, R. (1993) 'Biophilia, Biophobia and Natural Landscapes', in Kellert, S. and Wilson, E.O. (eds) *The Biophilia Hypothesis*. Washington: Island Press.

Valentine, G. (1996) 'Children Should be Seen and Not Heard', *Urban Geography*, Vol. 17(3), 205–220.

Valentine, G. (1997) '"Oh Yes I Can" "Oh No You Can't": Children and parents' understanding of kids' competence to negotiate public space safely', *Antipode* 29(1), 65–89.

Valentine, G. (2004) *Public Space and the Culture of Childhood*. Aldershot: Ashgate.

Valentine, G. and McKendrick, J. (1997) 'Children's Outdoor Play: Exploring parental concerns about children's safety and the changing nature of childhood', *Geoforum*, Vol. 28(2), 219–235.

Vanderbeck, R. and Dunkley, C. (2003) 'Young People's Narratives of Rural-Urban Difference', *Children's Geographies*, Vol. 1(2), 241–259.

Vanderbeck, R. and Dunkley, C. (2004) 'Introduction: Geographies of exclusion, inclusion and belonging in young lives', *Children's Geographies*, Vol. 2(2), 177–183.

Van Vliet, W. (1983) 'Children's Travel Behaviour', *Ekistics*, Vol. 50, 298.

Veitch, J. Bagley, S., Ball, K. and Salmon, J. (2006) 'Where do Children Usually Play? A qualitative study of parents' perceptions of influences on children's active free-play', *Health and Place*, Vol. 12, 383–393.

Waiton, S. (2001) *Scared of the Kids*. Sheffield: Sheffield Hallam University.

Wallenius, M. (1999) 'Personal Projects in Everyday Places: Perceived supportedness of the environment and psychological well-being', *Journal of Environmental Psychology*, Vol. 19(2), 131–143.

Ward, C. (1978) *The Child in the City*. London: Penguin Books.

Ward, C. (1990) *The Child in the Country*. London: Bedford Square Press.

Wells, N. (2000) 'At Home with Nature: Effects of "greenness" on children's cognitive functioning', *Environment and Behaviour*, Vol. 32(6), 775–795.

Wells, N. and Evans, G. (2003) 'Nearby Nature: A buffer of life stress among rural children', *Environment and Behaviour*, 35(3), 311–330.

Wells, N. and Lekies, K. (2006) 'Nature and the Life Course: Pathways from childhood nature experiences to adult environmentalism', *Children, Youth and Environments*, 16(1), 1–24.

Wheway, R. and Millward, A. (1997) *Facilitating Play on Housing Estates*. Joseph Rowntree Foundation: York.

White, R. (2004) 'Young Children's Relationship with Nature: It's importance to children's development and the earth's future', White Hutchinson Leisure and Learning Group, available online at: www.whitehutchinson.com/children/articles/nature.shtml (accessed 26/05/06).

White, R. and Stoeklin, V. (1998) 'Children's Outdoor Play and Learning Environments: Returning to nature', White Hutchinson Leisure and Learning Group, available online at: www.whitehutchinson.com/children/articles/nature.shtml (accessed 26/05/06).

Wild About Play (2004) www.playwork.co.uk/wildaboutplay/spaces.htm (accessed 26/05/06).

Williams, R. (1976) *Keywords: A vocabulary of culture and society*. Glasgow: William Collins. Cited in Mergan, B. (2003) 'Children and Nature in History', *Environmental History*, Vol. 8 (4).

Wilson, E.O. (1984) *Biophilia*. Cambridge: Harvard University Press.

Wilson, E.O. (1993) 'Biophilia and the Conservation Ethic', in Kellert, S. and Wilson, E.O. (eds) *The Biophilia Hypothesis*. Washington: Island Press.

Wilson, R. (2001) *'A Sense of Place'*, EE News, Vol. 18, no. 2, 2–7.

Worpole, K. (2003) *No Particular Place to Go*. Birmingham: Groundwork Trust.

Wridt, P. (2004) 'An Historical Analysis of Young People's Use of Public Space, Parks and Playgrounds in New York City', *Children, Youth and Environments*, 14(1), 86–106.

Zeiher, H. (2003) 'Shaping Daily Life in Urban Environments', in Christensen, P. and O'Brien, M. (eds) *Children in the City*. London: RoutledgeFalmer.

Appendix 1

Background to the review

As the opening exploration of the theme 'Play, naturally' indicates, there are two broad interconnected strands:

- children's play as a natural, instinctive behaviour
- children's preference for playing in natural sites.

These two themes provide the starting point for reviewing relevant research reports, academic texts and refereed journals. In developing this we recognise that we are not simply cataloguing all the available material relevant to the theme (which given the complexity of the task would be impossible) but are attempting to review the significant work with insight; to provide a picture of the state of knowledge and of the major issues in the area being investigated (Bell, 2005).

Inevitably, the experiences of the two reviewers have a significant impact on the approach and structure of this review. As such, much of the research included in this review is taken from an extended piece developed for a third year BA Playwork module at the University of Gloucestershire (Lester, 2005) and from involvement in the Wild About Play project and associated network of organisations supporting children's access to natural sites (Maudsley, 2005).

Also we are mindful that the two interconnected themes are highly complex. As Prout (2005:144) acknowledges, the period of childhood is not a unitary phenomenon, but consists of heterogenous materials that are 'cultural, biological, social, individual, historical, technological, spatial, discursive ... and more'. Childhood may be seen as a multiple set of constructions that arise and fall, connect and disconnect across these materials. To understand these requires moving beyond the dualisms of child/adult, indoor/outdoor, nature/culture, past/present, etc. to trace the connections and mediations across these materials to appreciate the nature of contemporary childhoods. Prout suggests that this requires an 'interdisciplinary' approach that crosses boundaries.

From this perspective, we have attempted to situate this review across a range of disciplines. In undertaking this, the primary focus has been to explore key research studies within the last ten years. However it is apparent that there are older significant theoretical perspectives frame much of this research.

We have used a number of key approaches in collecting materials for this review:

- Identifying significant published work and tracing references cited in the text. For example, a useful starting point for the review has been the collection of writings by Kahn and Kellert (2002), providing a valuable introduction to many of the key writers who have explored the relationship between children and nature. From this, we have been able to follow a number of significant strands.
- Academic journal search using key words associated with the theme using library databases – including Ingenta, SwetsWise, ScienceDirect, Blackwell and Wiley InterScience.
- Search of key periodicals including:
  - *Children's Geographies*
  - *Childhood*
  - *Childhood and Society*
  - *Children's Environments Quarterly*
  - *Children, Youth and Environments*
  - *Environment and behaviour*
  - *Journal of Environmental Psychology.*
- Internet search – using key words in Google and Scholar Google to identify significant and relevant sites.

Given the time constraints for this review, we appreciate that it cannot be a definitive and comprehensive study. However, we have been able to identify contemporary research relevant to the key themes and also to establish a historical context by tracing significant concepts and models that have been and are still influential and relevant to studying children's playful relationships with their local environments. Where appropriate, we have woven materials from these earlier studies into the review.

As Conway et al. (2004:2) expresses, 'the playing child interacts with a system that has echoes that stretch back millennia'. An understanding of the play process will contain 'ideas of evolution and adaptation, of environment and ecology, of deep laws, of nature and nurture, of genes and inheritance, of emotional repertoires, of identity and self'. We hope that this review offers a glimpse of this process of children playing naturally.

Collectively the results from this review enable us to outline some clear findings from the materials.

Appendix 2

Independent mobility and affordance

Kytta (2002, 2004) further develops the concept of affordance (Gibson, 1979/1986; Heft, 1989) to explore the interrelationship between independent mobility and the opportunity to actualise affordances within the local environment. This approach provides a useful framework for considering qualities of child-friendly spaces.

Independent mobility is considered to be an important factor in being able to use the potential offered in local spaces (Moore, 1986). Huttenmoser and Degen-Zimmerman (1995) note that five-year-olds who played independently in their neighbourhood had a richer and wider repertoire of play behaviours and activities.

Decisions about independent mobility of children are complex – they represent parental and societal concerns, and children's own sense of place and agency, etc. (as discussed in Part 3 of the review).

In looking at the potential of an environment to support a child's play, using the concept of affordance, we may see that a child perceives the environment while at the same time perceives themselves acting in this environment – a possibility of action aligned with their own needs, personality, motivations, etc. From this, Kytta (2004) proposes a series of levels:

Potential affordances: specified relative to an individual and in principle able to be perceived. Kytta states that the set of potential affordances of an environment is infinite. In any complex space we may be able to identify limitless possibilities for doing things.

Actualised affordances: the actual things the individual perceives, utilises or shapes. 'Actualised affordances are revealed through actions of the individual, or through self-report' (Kytta, 2004:181).

In exploring the notion of actualised affordances, Kytta outlines a range of 'subsets' to identify how personal, social and cultural qualities impact on perception, utilisation and shaping of affordances.

Field of promoted action: culturally defined and socially approved, this field marks and regulates which affordances can be actualised as well as the time, manner and place of actualisation. Affordances are carried out in a socially approved way.

Field of constrained action: as well as promoting the actualisation of affordances, it is possible to limit and constrain the process either through direct prohibition or through the design of spaces and objects so that not all users are able to actualise the potential affordances.

Field of free action: Kytta (2004:182) refers to this as an 'independent' discovery of affordances. Even though children might have been promoted into making affordances, there always exist affordances that children will make on their own:

> *The quality and quantity of the individual's independently actualised affordances vary according to the development of his perceptual, motoric and social skills in context. In addition, the personality traits, personal preferences and skills of the individual may have an effect on the independent discovery of affordances.*

Using this taxonomy, Kytta produced a model of hypothetical settings based on qualitatively different types of children's environments (2004:183):

Bullerby: the ideal setting where there is high level of independent mobility and affordances are utilised and shaped by children.

Glasshouse: here there is a large field of constrained range, but the environment is perceived as being rich. As such, the area may be fascinating and appears full of potential affordances, but this is not actualised because of restricted independent mobility.

Wasteland: here there is a limited field of constraint, but the environment itself has a reduced perceived and actualised affordance value and where independent mobility reveals the 'dullness' of the environment.

Cell: where there is a restricted field of free and promoted action and this makes it impossible for children to explore the potential affordances of their immediate environments and so children are not aware of the outside world and its potential.

In developing and applying this model, Kytta (2004:184) recognises that this 'ideal' scheme is inevitably influenced by the individual experiences and way of life of children:

> *The same physical environment can appear as a Bullerby-type environment to one child and as a cell-type to another. The physical, social and cultural environments form an inseparable entity, the adaptation to which is partly dependent on a child's individual characteristics.*

Appendix 3

Criteria for friendship with place

Chatterjee (2005) proposes an approach to considering child-friendly spaces by combining key elements of geography, environmental behaviour and environmental psychology with criteria for friendship. Starting with Hartup's (1991) key friendship qualities of reciprocity and commitment, Chatterjee uses Doll's (1996) definitions of friendship to locate key emerging concepts. The following table summarises these connections (adapted from Chatterjee, 2005:15).

Criteria for friendship (Doll, 1996)	Conditions of friendship	Proposed conditions for friendship with place	Emerging concepts
Mutual affection and personal regard	The ways in which each friend demonstrates a caring role with each other	Children will care for a place that: Holds them from harm when given the opportunity to maintain the place in some way (Hart, 1997). Provides a safe environment from traffic. Allows the child to satisfy physical needs.	Environmental care – children respect and care for places that are safe – sites of restoration (Kaplan and Kaplan, 1989; Bixler et al., 2002; Wells and Leckies, 2005)
Shared interests and activities	Represents the time and attention to have fun together	Place and child share a wide range of activities and interests through affordance and intrinsic qualities of the place	Place-child exchange and activity spaces (Gibson, 1986; Kytta, 2004; Fjortoft, 2001)
Commitment	The desire of both friends to continue fostering the relationship over time	The place offers a diverse and changing range of environmental resources, allows actualisation of affordances. (Nicholson, 1971; Kaplan and Kaplan, 1989; Fjortoft and Sageie, 2000)	The ability to maintain continuous reciprocal relationship with a place leads to discovering nested and sequential affordances of features – environmental learning and competence

Criteria for friendship (Doll, 1996)	Conditions of friendship	Proposed conditions for friendship with place	Emerging concepts
Loyalty	The intention of the friends to protect and look after each other	A sense of attachment in which allows the child to own or defend the space (Childress, 2004)	Place allows creation of a recognised and 'owned' space over time.
Self-disclosure and mutual understanding	Each child acquires and contributes to a unique understanding of each other	A place which allows children to manipulate and create their own special places (Dovey, 1990; Sobel, 1993)	Self-regulation of feelings, creating secret places (Korpela et al., 2002)
Horizontality	Friends share power in the relationship	A place that promotes the fields of free and promoted action, affordances are realised and the constraint of action is minimised (Kytta, 2004)	Freedom of expression, the child has a sense that they can create the world (Cobb, 1977)

Figure A3.1

Appendix 4

Nature values

Kellert (1996, 2002) proposes nine perspectives, or values, that describe the human relationship with the natural world. These 'values' are said to make up 'weak biological tendencies' to affiliate with natural processes and associated diversity of experience, collectively referred to as *biophilia* (Kellert, 2002:130). The phrase 'weak biological tendencies' suggests that the values have some adaptive purpose in human evolution, but the function and occurrence of these values is mediated through development and culture. The claim is made that the presence and content of these values will vary in individuals and societies, but that this variability is biologically framed. Kellert suggests that an imbalance in these values, either through omission or through an over exaggeration of specific perspectives would be dysfunctional and maladaptive.

Each value can be seen to make a contribution to the overall survival of the child in their immediate environments. In looking at these values, we may see how they reflect the benefits of the playful relationship between children and nature as described above. There may also be links between the perspectives outlined by Kellert and the play mechanisms proposed by Hughes (Play Wales, 2002).

Perspective	Description	Potential function/significance
Utilitarian	The biological advantage gained by humans through their exploration and exploitation of natural resources – food, clothing, shelter, tools, etc.	Physical and material security, self-confidence and self-esteem through playing with natural elements, recognition of relationship with natural systems and processes
Naturalistic	The satisfaction that humans derive from their contact with nature	Exploration, discovery, imagination, greater calm and coping strategies
Ecologistic-scientific	The motivation to study the biophysical patterns, structures and functions of the natural world	Intellectual competence, critical thinking, problem solving skills, enhanced capacity for observation and analysis

Perspective	Description	Potential function/significance
Aesthetics	The preference for natural designs over artificial, human designs	An ability to perceive patterns, recognise order and organisation, harmony, balance and symmetry
Symbolic	Refers to humans' use of nature symbols to communicate	Classifying and labelling abilities, enhanced communication and discourse though use of imagery and symbol
Humanistic	The human experience of a deep emotional connection with the sentient aspects of nature and its individual elements	Instrumental in developing intimacy, trust, enhancing self-confidence and esteem
Moralistic	A strong feeling of affinity and sense of ethical responsibility for the natural world	Developing a sense of underlying meaning and order, the desire to look after nature, enhanced sociability from shared moral and spiritual convictions
Dominionistic	The desire to master and control the natural world	Safety and protection, independence and autonomy, the urge to explore, willingness to take risks, show courage
Negativistic	Refers to negative affect associated with nature experiences including fear, aversion, disgust	Avoiding harm and injury, minimising risk

Figure A4.1   Kellert's perspectives describing the human relationship with nature (adapted from Kellert, 2002)

Qualities of attractive play spaces

Noren-Bjorn (1982) proposed principles for establishing the functional value of play spaces, recognising that these principles would form a 'qualitative value system where many combinations are possible and where one cannot state unequivocally what is "good"', a recognition that a range of choices and wide potential are at the heart of the play space. Thus, in planning for children's playgrounds and informal play spaces, the following factors should be considered.

Time: a place where play can last a long time, where it can be interrupted and then started again, where there is a wide range of space and materials available to all, where children can determine the start and ending times for their play.

Development: where children can make use of the materials and equipment according their level of development and needs, where materials can be manipulated in an endless variety of different ways according to needs, where there are new experiences available, new challenges, etc. As such, the space should continually offer the promise of more to come.

'Social' choice: where children can decide for themselves if they want to be together, play with others or want to be alone, where the accent is on co-operation, working time, comradeship, etc., in an accepting social and emotional environment, where children can share experiences of different ages and backgrounds, where individuality and diversity are openly valued, where children can negotiate, co-operate and resolve conflicts.

> *Closeness to other children of various ages gives the child a sense of the continuity of his own growth and development. The younger child can look ahead to what they will become. The older children can be childish when they need to, or they can serve as authority-figures and feel useful looking after and helping others.*
> (Noren-Bjorn, 1982:43)

Control: where children have the possibility to control space, explore and experiment, destroy and re-build, where children can have a real influence on their surroundings, both in making choices and decisions, and also being responsible for their environment.

Variety: where the environment provides a wide range of sensory and emotional experiences – smells, textures, sounds, heights, etc. – where there are new areas to explore, new challenges to face.

> *Different smells, rough and soft surfaces, warm and cold objects, beautiful and harsh sounds, sweet and bitter tastes all heighten the awareness of the world around us, especially when we are children.*
>
> (Noren-Bjorn, 1982:44)

Movement: where children have freedom of movement, both for their own personal movement (turning the world upside down, running, jumping, swinging, spinning, etc.) and movement within the environment (the freedom to go where they please), where the physical environment is varied and stimulating with different levels, uses, etc.

Identity: where the children's language and culture are respected and supported within their play, the child's language serves as a framework for its thoughts and should be continually developed. Where the children can develop their own ideas and self-expression through play and the processing of experiences assists the development of children's self-esteem and self-confidence.

> *Play serves as an aid to the child in dealing with his experience and overcoming problems and conflicts. Play can be a way to compensate for being little, work through a family conflict, handle the fear of being left alone, express anxiety about growing up. Play can help the child to deal with his sexual identity or provide an outlet for the wish to do something forbidden*
>
> (Noren-Bjorn, 1982:45)

Links to reality: where children become acquainted with the real world – its cultural and working life, where children see a variety of adult roles, where there are positive role models, where adults work co-operatively with each other, where children have the opportunity to join in with this world and the opportunity to take responsibility.

Freedom of choice: where children can choose freely on the basis of their own needs and desires what they want to do and with whom.

Dialogue and interaction: where children and adults can explore the world together, where they can share experiences on an equal basis, where children can lead and take control of the shared experiences without adults taking over.

In response to these conditions, Noren-Bjorn outlines the importance of a range of environmental factors:

Space for movement that encompasses wide ranging movements and space to be undisturbed.

Materials that invite physical exercise and challenge; for pretending, creation and construction, a range of loose materials to complement fixed equipment.

Variety of space, with different types of surfaces and ground cover, a space in which 'chance' can occur. By this, Noren-Bjorn (1982:188) refers to increasing natural elements wherever possible:

> *In a natural setting in a wood there are chance events occurring all the time: a bird flies away, a leaf falls, there is a rustling noise. The shape of stems and stumps can suddenly seem to resemble something else and so fire a child's imagination ... The more one finds, the more one discovers ... We have observed that it is often chance occurrences like the formation of a puddle that inspire children in their play. The bumpy or uneven or haphazard appeals to their fantasy and way of thinking. One could wish that playground planners would 'give chance to chance'.*